M000234311

The Journey to Spiritual Maturity

VOLUME 7

Growing in Holiness

Books in the Series

Volume One: The Challenging Road
Examines the nature of the journey itself.

Volume Two: Finding Our Purpose
Explores the five aspects of human purpose.

Volume Three: Overcoming Adversity
Deals with how God deepens us through adversity.

Volume Four: Learning to Love
Teaches us to love as God loves.

Volume Five: Transforming Faith
Inspires us to have a faith that can change the world.

Volume Six: Reason and Revelation
Encourages us to develop a systematic theology.

Volume Seven: Growing in Holiness
Helps us incorporate God's nature into our lives.

The JOURNEY To SPIRITUAL MATURITY

VOLUME 7

Growing in Holiness

Dr. Joel C. Hunter

with Timothy Davis

© 2001 by NORTHLAND, A CHURCH DISTRIBUTED

Published by NORTHLAND, A CHURCH DISTRIBUTED
530 Dog Track Road, Longwood, Florida 32750

Cover Design by Loyd Boldman
Book Design by Silent Planet

Special thanks to Steve and Georgia Bruton, Peggy Crosby, Ron Lawton,
Bob Towles, Jenni West, and Matt West.

All rights reserved. No part of this publication may be reproduced, stored
in a retrieval system, or transmitted in any form or by any means—elec-
tronic, mechanical, photocopy, recording, or any other—without the prior
written permission of NORTHLAND, A CHURCH DISTRIBUTED. The only
exception is brief quotations in printed reviews.

Except where noted otherwise, all Scripture quotations are from THE
NEW AMERICAN STANDARD BIBLE, Copyright © 1960, 1962,
1963, 1968, 1971, 1972, 1973, 1975, 1977 by the Lockman Foundation.
Scripture quotations noted NIV are from the HOLY BIBLE, NEW
INTERNATIONAL VERSION, Copyright © 1973, 1978, 1984 by the
International Bible Society. Scripture quotations noted NKJV are from the
HOLY BIBLE, NEW KING JAMES VERSION, Copyright © 1984 by
Thomas Nelson, Inc. Scripture quotations noted KJV are from the HOLY
BIBLE, KING JAMES VERSION, public domain.

Printed and Available through:
FIRSTPUBLISH, INC.
170 Sunport Ln. Suite 900
Orlando, FL 32809
407-240-1414
www.firstpublish.com

CONTENTS

Growing in God's Nature

"… as obedient children, not conforming yourselves to the former lusts, as in your ignorance; but as He who called you is holy, you also be holy in all your conduct, because it is written, "Be holy, for I am holy."

—*1 Peter 1:14–15*

PREFACE

*T*here may be nothing that draws more of us to the Christian faith than watching holy people live out their daily lives. The more closely we watch, the more interested we become. The differences we see demonstrated between those who believe in Christ and those who do not engage us both spiritually and emotionally. Our attention and our hearts are drawn to their witness. In reality, it is God, Himself, who builds within us the desire to be holy, and He loves using believers to get our attention.

This book is the seventh in a ten volume series entitled *The Journey to Spiritual Maturity.* The series is devoted to exploring the process by which Christians grow from spiritual infancy to spiritual maturity. We have likened this process to a journey—which began at the cross of Christ and which will be completed when we see God face to face in heaven. The goal of this journey is to become increasingly "conformed to the image of [God's] Son" (Romans 8:29), to become people of real spiritual depth and maturity.

In Volume One of this series, *The Challenging Road,* we sought to ground ourselves in fundamental truths of the Christian faith. We examined the nature of God, the depth of our own sinfulness, the glorious atonement of Christ, the mystery of our new life in Christ and the opposition we can expect to receive from the devil. In doing so, we prepared ourselves for the many challenges we would face along the road to spiritual maturity and we fixed our hope on the great rewards that lay in store for us at the journey's end.

Finding Our Purpose, was the emphasis of Volume Two. By examining five areas of purpose for which God created us—LIFE, LABOR, LIMITS, LEARNING, and LOVE—we learned how each of these spheres of life would be affected and deepened by our journey to maturity.

The third book in this series, *Overcoming Adversity,* sought to show us how God actually uses the attacks of Satan to accomplish our ultimate good. That gave us a security and hope as we moved into the fourth year of our spiritual journey together.

In Volume Four, *Learning to Love,* we read the Bible as a love story and began "to grasp how wide and long and high and deep is the love of Christ" (Ephesians 3:18 NIV). By understanding that our magnificent God first loved us, we learned to give our love to others more completely.

By the time we had reached the fifth year of our journey we were ready to step out with the confidence that God could use us to make a difference in the lives of others. *Transforming Faith* called us to expand our faith so that the world could be changed.

Volume six, *Revelation and Reason,* encouraged us to develop a systematic theology by gathering information about God from sources including, but extending beyond religious writings. We were encouraged to both see and love God in the world—not just in the church. The book helped us think well and praise better.

Now, in this volume, we are ready to examine what it means to live a holy life. We will be freed from striving to live perfectly as we come to understand that our holiness results only from Christ's character being displayed within us.

Planning Ahead

"… the road to holiness necessarily passes through the world of action."

—*Dag Hammarskjold, Markings*

INTRODUCTION

*S*hrouded by a thin blanket of clouds, the stars bled
pale light from the heavens to the earth below. At
times, the awesome brilliance of a lone star pierced
through the frigid darkness, but it provided little hope for the
desperate scene beneath. The ocean, mirror smooth and rolling
endlessly, reflected the mood of the heavens in its stillness.
Bearing the weight of triumph and tragedy, it too would fall
short of hope for the dying souls riding atop its crest. Along
with the stars, its declaration of peace and majesty would
drown silently amidst the cries and pleadings of the passengers
aboard the Titanic. Early morning on the deck of the mighty
ship, pounding feet and sounds of urgency assaulted the quiet-
ness like a thunderclap in the calm of sleep. Men and women,
clutching their loved ones and possessions, fought frantically
against the ever-increasing incline of the deck beneath their
feet as they continued searching for another way to safety.

Scattered throughout the deck, jewelry, furs, diamonds,
money, and other priceless possessions were destined for
descent to the bottom of the Atlantic. Some people grabbed

them, hoping to "cash in" the day they arrived safely home. Others considered them worthless and pushed their way toward the few remaining lifeboats. One woman who had waited patiently for a lifeboat in the midst of the curses, screams, and shoves finally reached the front of the line. An officer quickly helped her onto the boat. Sitting at last, she breathed a sigh, and as she did, it felt like icy needles stabbed her lungs. She cried while her eyes, dark and vacant, surveyed the scene around her. The activity and images were surreal. Shadowy figures merged, darted, and vanished against a backdrop of flickering yellow lights. Sounds seemed distant, almost unrecognizable. A few moments passed before she noticed a hand on her knee. It was a touch from a dear friend, who had arrived earlier to the lifeboat. Her friend's face was streaked with tear-forged lines that appeared ghostlike in the dim light. "We will survive this," her frightened friend said as she patted her leg.

Then suddenly the woman lifted her friend's hand, stood and focused her sight beyond the restless crowd. "Oh dear! Please, save my seat. I must retrieve something from my quarters." The friend nodded hesitantly as she folded her hands in prayer on her lap.

Squeezing her way through the mob of people, she dashed for the ship's interior, which by this time contained all sorts of debris. Broken chairs, plants, glass, personal items and other paraphernalia had fallen off shelves or crashed into walls and were strewn everywhere. She raced down the stairs and toward the middle of the ship. As she reached her hallway, a horrifying snap thundered through the air. The boat pitched, upsetting her balance and tossing her against a wall. A deep moan emanated from the ship. It was almost as though it too was experiencing fear and pain. She stood up, located her room and threw the door open. After grabbing her possession she dodged through the debris, ran over the slippery floors and arrived on the upper deck. Finally outside, she spotted her lifeboat, still waiting faithfully. Once again, she pressed through the people and reached the boat. Inside, she collapsed next to her friend. Immediately, the signal sounded to lower the boat. Ropes and pulleys rubbed and squealed while anxious eyes watched the boat slowly descend toward the icy waters.

"What did you forget? What on earth could be so important that you would sacrifice your position?"

Leaning closely and weeping softly she said, "I thought we might need these." Then opening the small brown bag that was hidden under her coat, she revealed several small oranges. In the darkness, her eyes met the eyes of her friend. "We've got to be prepared for the journey."

The sinking of the Titanic—most are familiar with the story of that catastrophic event. Dozens of additional stories have arisen from the experiences of the survivors. The preceding story is one that I came across some time ago. The sad truth of the Titanic was that its architects and builders actually believed that they had prepared for everything although clear flaws permeated the design of the ship. The alleged invincibility of the Titanic so pervaded their thinking that the ship earned the name, "Unsinkable." Unfortunately, because they expected absolute safety, they never prepared for disaster.

Many passengers continued sleeping, socializing, and strolling about though warned of the impending danger. Few people believed that the "unsinkable" Titanic would actually sink. By the time the severity of the situation set in, panic had erupted as the passengers noticed that most of the lifeboats had departed and were floating in the waters below. In desperation some jumped ship, plummeting eleven stories into the freezing waters, while the remaining people grasped tightly to the only thing that felt secure—the ship itself. At 2:20 a.m. on April 15, 1912, two hours and forty minutes after the collision, Titanic disappeared beneath the surface of the water, taking with it 1,500 lives.

The woman in our story, one of the 705 fortunate survivors, acted quickly and with relative focus. She wisely determined the most important valuable to bring was food. Other possessions, treasures before the catastrophe, turned to rubbish in light of the sinking truth. To the woman, only her life, her friend, and her sustenance became treasures. She prepared for that which offered hope and she lived.

The Titanic story is a powerful illustration for us as we begin this book, *Growing in Holiness*. It demonstrates that neither success nor failure depends upon how well we prepare, but upon the truth of preparation that is actually needed. Too often, the strides taken for holiness lure us in the opposite direction of God's holiness. Much like the architects of the Titanic, we prepare for holiness based on our own desires and goals rather than on what is truly beneficial. Ultimately, the holiness we construct cracks and sinks into the cold sea of our ignorance. That is a result of our failure to acknowledge that true holiness is God's, and only He can give it residence in our lives.

There is nothing more antithetical to the nature of man than God's holiness. Our first inclinations, our basic tendencies are utterly sinful and completely opposite of the holiness of God. Indeed, even our concept of God and His holiness falls woefully short of accurate. The truth is, the manner in which we conduct our lives grates hard against God's holiness.

In this book, we will discover the mysterious simplicity of the holiness of God. We will find that holiness is more than virtue of character. It is much more than self-discipline. It is more than pressing toward a spiritual goal. Holiness, as we will discover, is God's. While we are on earth, holiness will never be ours, only ours to share! As we explore this seldomly-charted territory, pray. We need to do that because God wants to hear from us. He really does. He also wants us to hear from Him. As He has throughout history, He yearns to open our hearts to experience His love. Now is the time to allow Him to mend our concepts of Him and His holiness.

Preparation
for Holiness

"There is such a thing as the danger of a selfish pursuit of holiness."

—*Gerald Vann, Eve and Gryphon*

*M*ost of us seldom think about *growing in holiness*. Rather, we run our day-to-day lives with "holiness on hold." Then when we tragically fail in a relationship, face unbearable temptation, or reap the rotten fruits of a poor choice, we begin to desire holiness. Feeling overwhelmed and hopeless, our cries rise up to God, "Oh, I just wish I could be holier, then I wouldn't be dealing with this!"

Certainly we need holiness at those times in our lives and certainly God wants us to run to Him for help and healing, but we really needed to be *growing in holiness* long before then. Waiting until we are in the midst of trials, with no resources available, is not the best time to get serious about holiness. That would be analogous to the captain of the Titanic inviting architects to return to the drawing board and rethink the design of the ship while thousands of gallons of seawater rush into the front bulkheads through a hull punctured by an iceberg.

To expect that we can put holiness on hold and still become spiritually mature is a misconception. True holiness is more than a conviction brought on by painful experiences and it certainly is not an immediate solution to a crisis. Unlike the instant effect of salvation, true holiness is rather a progressive work of God in man in which we aspire to sin less and less and become more and more like Christ. The theological term for this process is "sanctification." God can and will expand the capacity that each of us has for being holy.

Another misconception we have about *growing in holiness* is that we can accomplish it if we make it one of our New Year's resolutions. For example, we may reach a point in our lives when we look back and say, "Oh God, during the past year I've been more unholy than I should have been. This year I am going to trim off some self-indulgence, dishonesty, and a bit of gossip and slander. In fact, I am going to memorize ten Scripture verses a day, read through the Bible in a year, and do at least seven acts of kindness a week. That ought to do it!" Like the typical New Year's resolution, holiness becomes an attempt to clean up our acts to try to avoid the effects and pains caused by our sins. Although this may not necessarily be a bad thing to do, any assumptions we make that doing the right things—even the godly things—can make us holy and happy are false.

Hidden beneath such assumptions are beliefs that stem from a "works" mentality. These beliefs suggest that there are degrees to holiness, degrees to goodness, and degrees to success as Christians. The truth is, there is only one measurement of holiness and that is our closeness to God—and in many ways even that is up to God. Improving behavior will never make us holy or place us a notch above others. There is no amount of Scripture we can understand well enough, no quantity of wisdom we can gain, no number of acts we can perform, and no display of kindness we can emulate that will make us holy.

Consider this: In the heat of an argument we may voice some things to loved ones that are hurtful and maybe even downright hateful. Afterwards, when we have calmed down, we begin to feel convicted about our selfish behavior. At that point, we wonder what we can do to erase the words that we said and restore the relationships. Well, we could confess our sin to God and humbly approach those we offended and ask for forgiveness. In return, they might forgive us. However, even if that happens, can we be sure we have completely restored the relationships to their "pre-hurtful words" condition or erased what was spoken? Obviously, the answer is no! In order to experience God's love and the blessing of loving relationships we certainly must be involved daily in confession, repentance, and forgiveness. Nevertheless, we can do absolutely nothing to restore our lives completely from the damaging effects of our sins. Only God can do this in our lives and in the lives of others, both now and eternally; it does not happen through any efforts of our own. There is only one way to become holy and that is for God to make us holy.

Here are some questions worth pondering: Can we earn our salvation? Can we earn the privilege to enter heaven when we die? If we are able to earn our salvation or our positions in heaven, then why did Christ need to die? What goal did God have in mind when He left paradise to suffer and die on earth for us? The answer to all of these questions is that the Son of God had to give His sinless life as payment for our sins because we could never earn our salvation or ever pay the price ourselves.

Since our salvation is from Christ and not from ourselves, would He change the rules as they pertain to our growing in holiness? That is, after God draws us to Himself and saves us, would He then say, "Okay, now that I have saved you by My grace, you're on your own? You must grow in holiness (sanctification) by yourselves. You must earn my love by the things you do." Certainly, He would not ask that of us since we can never earn favor with God. However, if we have trusted Christ as our Savior then—according to God—we are holy in His sight and dearly loved.

God's Word gives us further proof: "It is God who works in you to will and to act according to His good purpose" (Philippians 2:13 NIV). Therefore, God is the One who prompts us, stirs us, and compels us to desire holiness. He is the One who helps us to act according to His nature and holiness that is already within us. If we have accepted Christ as Savior, His blood covers all of our past, present, and future sins.

> *There is only one way to become holy and that is for God to make us holy.*

The realization that should remove a tremendous weight from our souls is that the journey toward holiness includes the ultimate tour Guide (God). In addition, since we no longer live under the shackles of works and performance we may feel free to experience God in a whole new way. On the other hand, the fresh awareness of God's loving control over personal holiness may create a disturbing dilemma because of the significance we feel in being rewarded for performance. By performing better than others perform, we may believe that we are somehow superior to others. Both public and private accomplishments tend to produce great rewards and provide us with meaning. Yet, this performance mentality may actually prevent us from experiencing the pains of inadequacy that can help us to recognize our need for the holiness of God.

We cannot be a little bit holy; just like we cannot be a little bit pregnant or a little bit human.

Coming to terms with our inadequacy and our total depravity is a considerable challenge for us if we struggle with a "works" mentality. This is mainly because we live in a world where comparing and competing with one another is practically a pastime. The fact is, we are all unholy without God. With God, we are holy. There are no degrees of measurement and there is no middle ground. It is impossible to add to God's holiness. If we have been given a "new life in Christ" (II Corinthians 5:17), we cannot be a little bit holy; just like we cannot be a little bit pregnant or a little bit human. We are either pregnant or not, and either human or not. Holiness is not dependent on who we are; holiness depends on God's nature entering us. Holiness is something different from that which the world has generally understood.

The final misconception is a hedonistic holiness that focuses on growing in holiness as a means for personal improvement. Instead of laying aside our plans and goals to worship a perfect God on His holy hill, we end up presenting our wish list of ways we would like for Him to improve us. While we may recognize the sovereignty and saving grace of God, we often fail to accurately picture Him and recognize His transcendence. We live in a society that is increasingly arriving at the conclusion that man is the center of the universe, that we are the ones who are high and lifted up. Even the church has been captivated by this mentality.

The following humorous illustration addresses this issue of self-importance: Dogs look at their caregiver and think, "Wow! You feed me, pet me, keep me clean, and help me when I am sick. You must be a god!" Cats look at their caregiver and think, "Wow! You feed me, pet me, keep me clean, and help me when I am sick. I must be a god!" A misdirected focus on self-importance creates an elevated and false picture of self. Our central focus should not be on ourselves; it should be on God.

The aim of God's holiness, though endearing and transforming to us as individuals, focuses less on the needs and desires of individuals and more on the unity of His children. You see, God loves us personally. He loves us as individuals. He saves us as individuals. Nevertheless, He does not save us to remain individuals. God has always been interested in the family. God is a family man.

You may recall when God spoke to Abram in Genesis 12; He addressed him as an individual yet, He called him to be a great nation. His purpose for Abram extended beyond his individuality. When Jesus walked with Peter He loved him as an individual. Yet, when He looked at him He saw His church. His vision for Peter involved his relationship with the growing family of believers. When we read Chapter 7 in the book of Revelation about the worship that is occurring around the throne of God, we do not see individuals singled out; we see a family. In fact, the entire Bible is about people uniting to worship God and fulfill His purpose. Before His death, Jesus Christ prays to His Father: "that they (believers) may be one, even as We are One" (John 17:22). God wants our holiness to reflect His relationship with Jesus in our relationships with each other. God intends us to pursue that kind of closeness, that kind of love, and that kind of holiness. Therefore, the ultimate goal of a Christian is not just improving one's own personal life or character. True holiness has the character of God. We must seek holiness together and for God's purpose. If we are to become more like Christ, we cannot do it alone!

Understanding Holiness

I have demonstrated several crucial elements in our search for holiness, including our need for God's holiness in our lives, the necessity of preparing well for His holiness, and our inability to attain holiness by our own efforts. In the following chapters, we will learn much more about how to grasp and understand the power of holiness.

Holiness is really a treasure, one that God desires for us to possess. This treasure, however, may be buried deep beneath our misconceptions and isolation. It is important that we grasp this revelation of God's holiness. Otherwise, we may walk away from this book with a one-sided view—knowing about the treasure of holiness, but not having it in our possession. We may walk away still believing that holiness is something we have to do or that it is simply yielding to God.

Before further examining this treasure, let us consider how we feel about sharing a kind of closeness in which someone else sees and knows our every strength and weakness. We would probably be hesitant because there is a tremendous amount of responsibility attached to being totally unified with another. In this world, most of us feel separated from each other and from God. Since the fall of man, we have continued to develop the characteristics that result from our being away from God. We may spend most of our lives just floundering around, isolated and lost.

We live in a society that is increasingly arriving at the conclusion that man is the center of the universe, that we are the ones who are high and lifted up.

There is an excellent analogy depicting our condition. It is a story about a farmer who tried to save the life of a small bird during a cold winter:

One Christmas Eve, a very nice and respectful farmer sent his family off to church. The whole story of God coming to earth as a man just did not make sense to him and so, not wishing to be a hypocrite, he stayed home. As he was adding logs to the fireplace, he heard one thump, and then another, on the window. He looked through the window to see a dazed bird flopping around in the snow. He figured that the bird had seen the fireplace glowing and was trying to get near it for warmth. The window had interrupted the bird's plan. Worried that the bird might freeze to death, the farmer thought he would try to get it into his barn; so after watching the bird for several minutes, he slipped into his coat, put on his hat, and trudged outside. It had snowed for days and the ground, along with everything in sight, glistened white in the moonlight. He trudged out to the barn and opened the barn doors. The light and warmth spilled outside into the cold night air. The bird had regained its senses by now, but was not at all interested in entering the barn.

Determined to help the poor creature, the farmer walked into the barn, grabbed a handful of grain from a sack and dribbled it all the way from the barn to the little bird. His hopes of the bird following the food trail into the barn were dashed as the bird continued to hop aimlessly. Now he was concerned that the bird was going to freeze to death. He thought aloud, "If only I could become a bird for a moment, I could lead him to safety." Right then, the church bell rang. As it rang out, he realized why God had to become a man.

> *The word holy actually means separate or set apart for God's service. In other words, holiness is profoundly different from that which the world offers every day.*

When Jesus Christ enters our lives, calls us by name, and offers safety through unity beyond our wildest dreams, we cower or flee. Although we are terribly lonely and yearning for companionship, we desperately crave and even demand independence. While we are scared and cry out for safety, we ruthlessly defend our space at all costs. Though we are hope-starved and searching for real answers, our suspicious nature prevents us from believing in anything. To actively unite with God means tearing ourselves away from our purposeful yet decaying self-reliance and becoming vulnerable in a perilous way.

Growing in holiness demands that we surrender all of our trust and hope to the One who is truly holy, while humankind impels us to believe in no one but ourselves. Still, our reluctance and resistance is not unusual. To the secular world, surrendering to something like holiness is simply crazy—trusting in a God who can neither be seen nor heard is just absurd! Holiness is out of the ordinary. In fact, the word holy actually means separate or set apart for God's service. In other words, holiness is profoundly different from that which the world offers every day.

Present Matters

Recently, I flew to Ohio to visit my father. Totally blind and nearly deaf, he now lives in a nursing home just a mile from my sister's residence. The window of time that I have to be with him is closing daily. Whenever I see him, I tell him about his grandkids, the family, and a variety of matters of significance to him in the past. To tell you the truth, sometimes I do not think he knows who I am, but he appreciates the company.

Before leaving Florida, I had shared with my son, Isaac, a college student at Taylor University in Indiana, that I would be making the trip to visit my dad. Isaac mentioned that he had a big test on Thursday. I said, "No problem—I probably couldn't get over to Taylor this time anyway, because this is going to be a quick visit."

To my surprise, on Friday, Valentine's Day, Isaac knocked on the front door of my sister's house. I could hardly believe it, "Isaac, what are you doing here?"

He stepped inside and gave me a big hug. "I borrowed a car," he replied as he noted the expression on my face. "Come on Dad, you were only a couple of hours away and I just wanted to be with you, that's all."

Why would he do something like that? Because he wanted to demonstrate to his friends his undying devotion to his father? Nah, Because he could not find anything better to do? Yeah, right—it was Valentine's night and he could have been out on a date. You know what, I just took him at his word— he wanted to be with me! Imagine that.

Close Call

Why does God desire us to grow in holiness? Is it because He wants us to be godly examples? Well, yes, however, that is not the primary reason. Is it because He knows it will bring joy and fulfillment to our lives? Of course, but His desire is much deeper than that. Is it because He is a holy God who hates sin of all kinds? Yes, but His loving desire is greater than that as well. Is it because He desires to teach us about Himself, His ways, and His path toward spiritual maturity? Absolutely, but there is much more to His desire for holiness than our growth. The primary reason that God desires for us to seek holiness is potentially the most liberating truth of all: God just wants to be with us! It is that simple and that pure. Our pursuit of holiness is not a case of need or a case of His expec- tations, but a case of relationship. The core of God's desire for us involves pursuing a deep, growing intimate relationship with Him. He simply wants to be with us.

When we give the holiness of God considerable thought, I believe that it frightens us. That is partly because it is beyond our comprehension, and partly because it reminds us of our unavoidable inadequacies and failures to measure up. Therefore, in order to contain it we place our concept of God in a box. We cannot understand how a Creator-God can be all powerful, all knowing, jealous, perfect, holy, demanding, unyielding, and unseen, while at the same time, being tender, all loving, merciful, intimately involved, caring, gentle, sacrificial, and patient. It just does not make sense to us! Therefore, we often choose to focus on the truth and power of the mighty God who parted the Red Sea and destroyed Sodom and Gomorrah, rather than the love and grace of an endearing God who willingly sacrificed His life for us just to be with us again. In other words, we select the attributes of God we want Him to have. We forget the God who misses us dearly and who longs to hold us, yet we remember the God who is perfect, holy, and repulsed by sin.

> *The primary reason that God desires for us to seek holiness is potentially the most liberating truth of all: God just wants to be with us!*

Holiness means different, other, and separate, but we use the world's methods in attempt to achieve it. Those methods are ineffective when it comes to growing in holiness. Holiness does not say, "Be busy in order to accomplish." It does not say, "Try harder! Burn out for God!" God is not a distant being in heaven coaching us along by yelling, "I know you trust in Me, but if you want something, you're going to have to make it happen by your own effort." Those are lies! They create bondage and inhibit the freedom that God has given us.

Holiness never demands that we achieve by our own effort. God wants a relationship. He wants to work in us. That is what we have to understand about Him and His holiness. He invites us to be with Him, neither to achieve for Him nor to try to be perfect for Him. It is in the process of being with Him that perfection comes. We, like God, have the natural desire for relationships and intimacy. He is our Father. We are His children. In other words, we are family.

In the following chapter, we will continue the theme of preparing for God's holiness—revealing key ways to develop intimacy with God. While God will never love us more or know us more than He does right now, there are some important steps we can take to increase our closeness to Him. My prayer is that we would surrender to Him and allow His Spirit to draw near to us. The journey toward holiness begins with our yielding to Him and simply being with Him.

Provision
of Holiness

*"A holy person is one who is sanctified by the presence and
action of God within him."*

—*Thomas Merton, Life and Holiness*

CHAPTER TWO

*W*e all crave closeness, especially that which results in intimacy. From infancy to old age our lives are filled with relationships that intrigue us, challenge us, and provide us with love, meaning, and even pain. Through these relationships our growth is affected physically, psychologically, socially, and spiritually. Whether we are rich or poor, young or old, powerful or weak, self-seeking or actively benevolent, all of us must rely on others in one way or another. Even our highly exalted view of independence cannot confine our deep indwelling need for closeness with others. It pervades nearly every aspect of our lives.

However, while we crave intimate relationships with others, we also fear having our true feelings, desires, thoughts, and sins exposed. This is the dilemma—our unquenchable desire for closeness is matched only by our fear of being known. We may face this same predicament in a relationship with God and a way out of it does not come easily.

In response to the intense conflict within, some of us try to slip into a place from which we can survey our surroundings and at the same time feel safe. We find comfort in these trenches. With our fears temporarily appeased and our desires partially satisfied, we feel close enough to God to experience His blessings but far enough away to remain in control. Life in the trenches, however, is far from abundant. When we avoid a deep relationship with Him, we fall short of fully appreciating the reason for His presence in our lives: the joy of a wonderful, personal relationship with Him. Nestling into our trenches, our focus becomes more on receiving from God or performing for Him rather than on seeking His holiness. In turn, the very thing that we desire and need—God's closeness—is kept at a distance. Why do we choose to live in the trenches when we can dwell in the palace of God? I believe we do it because we assume it is easier.

Drawing near to Him requires our obedience and our willingness to discard our faulty ways of doing things in order to follow God's way.

The truth is, pursuing a relationship with God does require extraordinary courage and unfamiliar humility on our part. It demands a willingness to allow Him to reveal areas in our lives that need His intervention. Those areas, like festering wounds, are painful to expose and even more agonizing to touch. Welcoming His closeness demands that we diligently seek an accurate view of God and of ourselves—throwing aside our often self-focused and mistaken views. Drawing near to Him requires our obedience and our willingness to discard our faulty ways of doing things in order to follow God's way.

Most of us would rather remain in the trenches than go through that kind of discomfort. We would rather live in a spiritual "no man's land" than experience the pain of rising above our fears and our self-reliance. Staying there, however, will ultimately leave us longing and empty. Abandoning the trenches for God stimulates growth and joy in our relationship with Him. Therefore, do we want to merely endure the useless pain of our inaction and fear, or are we ready to allow God to move us toward Him with purpose? Either way we are going to experience pain, but our perspective of it and response to it will determine our growth.

James 1:2-4 reads, "Consider it all joy, my brethren, when you encounter various trials, knowing that the testing of your faith produces endurance. And let endurance have its perfect result, that you may be perfect and complete, lacking nothing." Instead of allowing pain to destroy us, God can use it to draw us closer to Him. Pain can compel us to yearn for His companionship and authority.

Growing deeper with God produces amazing freedom and joy. It has the potential to break through the veil of our fears and our limited understanding. Seeking intimacy with God will ultimately be more liberating for us than if we do not. Even in our pursuit of Him, He is actually the One who is working. He is the One who pulls us, moves us, and changes us. Our part is to lay aside our desires, our fears, and ourselves.

There are three important truths that enhance our relationship with God. In order to experience a rich closeness with Him, we must seek to incorporate them into our relationship with Him. Our relationship is enhanced through commitment, obedience, and knowledge.

Relating to God through Commitment

As we begin to yield to God and allow ourselves to be vulnerable with Him, we will start to experience a dramatic closeness to Him. That intimacy will deepen as we become more vulnerable with Him and dependent upon Him. Unfortunately, we are not accustomed to approaching intimacy in that manner. In fact, our mentality is often diametrically opposed to God's design. While we may believe that we are pursuing true intimacy, the basis of our effort is usually rooted in our own desires and driven by our fears.

For example, when a couple experiences problems within a marriage or a love relationship, the struggles are often viewed as signs of impending doom. Many couples will perceive relational difficulties as roadblocks directing them to detour and leave their relationships. But as those of us in healthy relationships know, couples who courageously burrow through the barriers of intimacy and experience the pain that may be involved are usually on the road to joy and success. On the other hand, those who avoid the difficulties associated with true intimacy and fail to work through them are invariably headed for disaster or despair. Usually, when their relationships end, they believe the primary reason was because they "weren't ready for that kind of commitment" or "just weren't right for each other." Whatever the response, their reason is usually centered on a belief that "getting ready" for a relationship will effectively eliminate problems in it. In truth, we can never fully "get ready" for a commitment to someone. Although preparation certainly helps, we cannot shelter ourselves from the struggles or joys of a growing intimacy.

What about our readiness to pursue God? What can we do to get ready for an intimate relationship with Him? What are the steps that we need to take to welcome Him into our lives? How much preparation is required to fully commit to a God who desires closeness, regardless of our strengths, weaknesses, and accomplishments? The Bible says that when we believe in Jesus Christ, we automatically become participants in a relationship with God. At the moment of our commitment, we begin working from within that relationship. While it is proper to look forward to holiness, we cannot prepare for a relationship with God. Rather, our readiness and the fruits of that relationship grow from our connection with God. They cannot be attained before we commit to Him, and they cannot simply be produced by our own will. In fact, as sinners we can neither qualify nor adequately get ready for a relationship with God.

As parents, did we feel ready for parenthood when our children started arriving? Were we qualified to become parents? Most of us did not have any idea what we were getting into. The truth is that we become parents and then spend the rest of our lives trying to qualify as good moms or dads.

Were we qualified when we were hired for the jobs we have now? We may have been qualified to get the jobs, but we were not necessarily qualified to do the jobs. This is why most jobs come with training. However, once employed, we spend the rest of our time at the jobs trying to qualify as good workers. Most of us serving in ministry were not qualified when God placed us in that particular arena. Nevertheless, God placed us there and we will spend the rest of our ministry trying to qualify for the calling. God is like that! He puts us into situations we are not qualified for and then He makes us ready while we are there.

The point is that we will never qualify for a relationship with God. We can never do enough or be enough to impress Him. In fact, taking into account our sinful nature, we are not qualified for any good service. However, God is and His qualified Spirit is in us. In Christ, we qualify. In Christ, we are ready. Because He loves us, He qualifies us in our relationship with Him.

> But we all, with unveiled face, beholding as in a mirror the glory of the LORD, are being transformed into the same image from glory to glory, just as from the LORD, the Spirit. (II Corinthians 3:18)

Notice that God is totally and completely responsible for changing us and making us ready. Since this transformation originates with God, our part is simply to recognize it. Our knowledge of God and our commitment to Him follow His call to us. Then as we mature and yield to Him, we begin to recognize more of His presence in us and His desires start to matter more to us than our own desires do.

Then as we mature and yield to Him, we begin to recognize more of His presence in us and His desires start to matter more to us than our own desires do.

Prior to that level of maturity, some of us may actually believe that we became Christians because we wanted to give up a sinful lifestyle. Surely getting what we wanted all of the time and becoming worn out with constantly satisfying our own needs and personal desires, disgusted us enough to turn to Him. Our selfishness and constant calculating how others could bless us are, we assume, what prompted us to accept Christ.

That is not the case. None of us comes to God for those reasons. God always comes to us. If it were up to us, we would always choose ourselves over God. Instead, God draws us, changes us, and prepares us even when we are not searching for Him.

Recently, I spoke with a member of our congregation who was formerly an exotic dancer. She told me how she became a Christian. One night while she was on stage at an adult nightclub, she saw someone she had never expected to see—Jesus Christ was standing about fifteen feet from her in the middle of the audience. She heard Him say, with absolutely no condemnation, "I want you for something better than this. I have got something far better for you." That night, she walked out of that place and never returned. She had not prepared for a visit from Christ. She had not readied herself for that kind of commitment, but God came to her and requested a commitment regardless of her lack of readiness and she yielded to Him.

Many of us are caught unprepared when a powerful and loving God enters our lives. We may be accustomed to experiencing His blessing, but the concept of a relational and intimate God is quite foreign to us. While we may recognize that He is a personal God, our experience of Him (even His blessings) distracts us from knowing Him personally. Frequently, we settle for pursuing His provisions, comfort, and instruction instead of actively seeking intimacy and closeness with Him. Some of us may attempt to get ready for God by fine-tuning our gifts or trimming back our sins.

Others of us may have given up altogether, finding at least a minimal peace in coasting through our spiritual lives. In a manner of speaking, we are so filled to overflowing with the spiritual "milk" of God's blessings that we do not crave the spiritual "meat" of God. Granted, God willingly showers us with His blessings. They are a part of who He is. However, His provision of blessings is not the purpose for His calling. Instead, those blessings are primarily intended to bring into focus His incomprehensible love for us and His supreme desire for intimacy with us. It is designed to catch our attention and draw us into a relationship with Him.

Thankfully, God does not wait for us to get ready for Him. Behind the scenes He pulls us closer and makes us ready. To respond we must attune our ears to His gentle calling and surrender. To resist will only cause us unnecessary pain. We can choose to "kick against the goads" as the Apostle Paul did before his conversion. That is, we can attempt to fight Him in our lives and in the lives of others, but to do so is futile. However, if we yield to Him we will discover an unfathomable and soul-changing relationship waiting to be explored. By heeding His call and committing to a close relationship with God—even if it is difficult at times—we can be ready to experience incredible blessings.

Relating to God through Obedience

When we were teenagers going out with friends for the evening, our parents would say, "Now, be good." They never said, "Be holy!" Yet God, as our eternal and perfect Parent, commands us to be holy. For sinful people (that would be us) that is a phenomenal and formidable calling. Still, even though something is difficult or unimaginable to attain, it does not mean we should not strive for it. As mentioned in the first chapter, our progression and preparation toward holiness will seem to be against our nature for an important reason: it is against our nature. It is far beyond our ability to achieve, yet it is a command of God. In Leviticus 11:45 He said, "For I am the LORD, who brought you up from the land of Egypt, to be your God; thus you shall be holy for I am holy."

In this society we are not well equipped to answer commands. In fact, most of us view God's law as the basis for discussion and interpretation rather than as the basis for action.

In this society we are not well equipped to answer commands. In fact, most of us view God's law as the basis for discussion and interpretation rather than as the basis for action. That is, we talk about God so that we can understand Him better; then if we understand, we may act. The problem is that we never come to a full understanding of God. How could we ever fully understand an omniscient God and His commandments? We have enough trouble understanding ourselves. To this day many of us are still trying to figure out how to work the television remote! Invariably, we will end up falling short of adequately understanding God's commandments or their purpose. Until we come to terms with our limitations in that area, we will end up bound by our own conceptions of Him. God's law, while it is His perfect will that we follow it, was also designed to bring into light our total depravity and need for Him. Seeking His calling to be holy is both His command and our acknowledgement of our desperate condition. Our reaction to God's command should only partly be to try to understand it, but it should primarily be to try to act on it.

In addition to our limited understanding of God, we have another problem. Life is not easy nor is it predictable or consistent. If you have children, there is no such thing as a predictable day. If you are involved in important relationships, at any moment one of those relationships could change for better or worse. However, even when life is uncertain and threatening to spin out of control, we have a sovereign God who is in control. By paying close attention to His leadership and guidance we will discover that the impossible can be accomplished. By obeying His commands we can experience freedom and hope within the chaos. The mentality of the world equates following God's commands with less freedom. In reality, heeding them actually provides more freedom, more understanding, and less discouragement for us. Obeying His commands draws us closer to Him and provides us with unfathomable blessings. Even though God's perfect commandments leave little room for our opinions, they are always the best for us.

It is important to remember that His commandments and our allegiance to them are all a part of a loving relationship with Him. Sometimes we lose ourselves in just doing the right things. We may choose to live under the law instead of in a relationship with God. Over time, that can cause us to become prideful, angry, or discouraged. If we focus only on obedience, our spiritual progress evolves into a kind of trophy that we use to measure and compare ourselves with others. In turn, obedience to God is replaced by self-righteousness. On the other hand God's law is always abundantly seasoned with love. He does not hold to the "moral ledger" of comparison.

It was in the eighteenth century that Benjamin Franklin developed the moral ledger concept. In addition to being viewed as a political founding father of America, he unfortunately could also be dubbed the "spiritual founding father" of many American Christians. Many of us still apply the moral ledger concept to our Christian walk—"If I just have enough good works over and against my bad works, then I can count myself as good enough." Although we are well aware of the truth of God's grace saving us, we continue to pursue our own righteousness, believing in its salvation and its ability to make us godly. However, our pursuit does neither. Instead, it creates a false sense of self by making us temporarily feel better about ourselves.

Contrary to Franklin's moral ledger, the Apostle Paul, one of the founding fathers of Christianity (through Jesus Christ), did not place his hopes on his fleshly deeds or his success in obeying God's commands. In Philippians 3:7-8, he says:

> But whatever things were gain to me, those things I have counted as loss for the sake of Christ. More than that, I count all things to be loss in view of the surpassing value of knowing Christ Jesus my LORD, for whom I have suffered the loss of all things and count them but rubbish in order that I may gain Christ.

Unlike Franklin, Paul viewed his relationship with Christ as his most treasured possession, over and above his many great deeds. His ability to follow commands only flowed out of a relationship with Christ. The same is true for us. While the good things we do have a powerful and positive effect on our lives and on the lives of others, they are the direct result of a relationship with Christ and His power at work within us.

In truth, all of our deeds are rubbish apart from a deepening relationship with God.

A while ago, I observed a perfect illustration of this truth. While reading by the pool at my apartment complex I had the opportunity to observe as a father taught his little girl how to swim. She clung to his neck in absolute terror. Patiently, he kept saying to her, "Look at me, honey. Look at me." Her large round eyes darted from his face to the water . . . his face to the water. Trying to calm her, he hugged her tightly and said, "I'm not going to let you go. I'm not going to drop you. I want you to trust me." She was too frightened to hear his words. Her arms encircled his neck. Finally, he said, "Honey, the water is not your enemy. If you do what I say, the water is what will hold you up."

Reflecting on the father's words, I began to realize that the same truth applies to us. If we have a relationship with our heavenly Father, clinging and trusting are what give us confidence to do His commandments, and His words will hold us up. When we choose to ignore His commands and willfully do things on our own, we struggle, experience fears, and encounter difficulties. More importantly, we end up delaying His work in our lives. Like the words of the father to his little girl, God's commandments are designed to provide hope and help to give us courage. By following them, we can avoid any negative consequences that would result from our disobedient or foolish actions. Of course, we still experience the pain of living in a sinful world. We are able though to regard our suffering as joy rather than the result of our defiance or ignorance. Still, regardless of our right or wrong actions, God is gracious, forgiving, and patient. His arms wrap tightly around us when we feel overwhelmed. He calmly speaks to us in words only our hearts can hear: "Look at Me. I am not going to drop you. I will get you through this. Trust in Me."

Relationship is the goal; blessings are the consequences.

Within a personal relationship with God, we are abundantly provided for and eternally protected. Holiness and obedience to His commands are all about His connection with us. The Bible says in Romans 8:32, "He who did not spare His own Son but delivered Him up for us all, how will He not also with Him freely give us all things?" What a passionate way to describe His love for us! He sacrificed His own Child to pay the penalty for our past, present, and future rebellion. Yet we were the ones who owed the debt. God's love for us is so extreme and beyond our comprehension, that through Jesus Christ He has chosen to hide our sins from His eyes. Therefore, when God holds us tightly, He not only sees us, but His Son, Jesus, whom He sacrificed for us. There is no way He is going to let us go. There is no way He is going to ignore us. There is no way He is going to hurt us. He offered His innocent Son for a relationship with us. So, once we enter into a relationship with Christ we are eternally secure within that relationship. Obeying His commandments then becomes a matter of loving God and choosing what is best. It is not that we are attempting to earn His favor or blessings, but that as we yield to Him and seek His will for our lives we will experience the inherent blessing of personal connection with Him. Relationship is the goal; blessings are the consequences.

Relating to God Through Knowledge

A young man called his father on the phone from college and said, "Dad, I just don't understand the physics course I'm taking."

The father said, "Son, I give you credit for just enrolling in that class. I know you took two years of physics in high school and did well, but college physics is an entirely different level. So, I just give you credit for trying."

The son became silent, so the father continued, "Why don't you ask your teacher to help you with the problem? I'm sure she'll explain it to you and you'll be fine."

The son stopped him short and said, "Uh, Dad, you don't understand. Even though I took physics in high school and made good grades, I never really understood it, I just memorized the formulas."

How many of you feel like you are living life merely by practicing the formulas? You have learned the details of "how to make it," but you have failed to capture the big picture. Maybe you know that you need to plug this in here and that in there, but your life really seems like a series of mechanical decisions. You have been trained. You know the facts. You have the information, but you still do not quite get it.

A French author, Sebastien-Roch Nocolas de Chamfort (1741-94) once wrote, "A man is not necessarily intelligent because he has plenty of ideas, any more than he is a good general because he has plenty of soldiers." In other words, what is important is not how much you have learned, but what you have learned—and to what end. We really need to shake off the mentality of just learning the facts for facts' sake and believing that is what learning is. That is not learning. In fact, it can be exactly the opposite. Like an overflowing junkyard, our minds can become cluttered and unproductive with too much useless knowledge. We may amass hordes of data on a variety of subjects, feel intelligent, and even apply our knowledge but to what end? Is it to be successful, happy, and safe in this world or to prepare ourselves and those around us for eternity? Knowledge that is truly knowledge is that which challenges, strengthens, and changes us. Ultimately, true knowledge is that which teaches us about God.

The acquisition of more and more information can be an obsession. Whether it is acquiring knowledge about facts, people, philosophies, religion, or ourselves, our obsession is evident by our restlessness in the midst of abundant information. Granted, God wants us to grow in knowledge and understanding. He has made us to be thinkers, both inquisitive and creative. Nothing at all is inherently wrong with gaining knowledge. Still, there is such a thing as pursuing the wrong kinds of knowledge.

For instance, if a man has a propensity toward over-involving himself in house projects to the neglect of his family, the last thing he needs to do is increase his knowledge of table saws by purchasing one for his workshop. His increased knowledge would only exacerbate his family problem. Or if a woman suffers from depression and has difficulty facing reality, the last thing she needs to do is drown herself in melodramatic novels. More than likely, the woman's increased knowledge would fail to free her from depression. Likewise, if a student is doing his homework and faithfully struggling to solve a complicated math problem, the last thing he needs is to be given the answer before he completes the task. His premature exposure to that information would not encourage his learning but hinder it. Certainly there is nothing inherently wrong with buying table saws, reading novels, or looking at the answer before solving a homework problem (assuming of course that the instructor gave permission to do so). But we must be careful and selective with the information we consume or it may consume us in the process. Our obsession with seeking knowledge has been around since the Garden of Eden. Sin first entered the world when we ate the fruit from the "tree of knowledge of good and evil"(Genesis 2:9b). From that point on, we began to crave more than what we had been given. We desired that which was off-limits; that which could destroy us.

For example, consider the mom who turns on the computer with the primary intention of locating information on the Internet about raising godly children. Enraptured by the abundance of information, by the time she has finished searching, she may be surprised to find herself wandering about web sites pertaining to offshore oil drilling or the art of origami—topics that had nothing to do with her primary goal. Hours can pass and the children may become the last thing on her mind. The Internet is filled with "links" to vast amounts of information, and it is all at our fingertips looking quite appealing. The pursuit of knowledge (for knowledge's sake), however, does have the potential to cause us harm and can steer us further from our true purpose. It can lure us away from relationships with others and from the most important relationship of our lives—our closeness with God.

God has always intended knowledge to link people to Him. In Luke 2 we are provided with a rare passage describing Jesus as a child. Tucked away within the passage is vital information illustrating the connection between our pursuit of knowledge and our relationship with God. At age twelve, like all Jewish boys, Jesus, along with His mother and father, attended a feast of the Bar Mitzvah. The festival represents a Jewish boy's transition into manhood. Returning from the festival, Joseph, who was with the caravan of men, thought that Jesus was with Mary. Mary, who was with the caravan of women and children, believed that Jesus was with Joseph. After discovering that He was missing, they traveled back to Jerusalem to find Him:

> And it came about that after three days they found Him in the temple, sitting in the midst of the teachers, both listening to them and asking them questions. And all who heard Him were amazed at His understanding and His answers. And when they saw Him, they were astonished; and His mother said to Him, "Son why have You treated us this way? Behold, Your father and I have been anxiously looking for You." And He said to them, "Why is it that you were looking for Me? Did you not know that I had to be in My Father's house?" (Luke 2:46 – 49)

Notice how Jesus links intellectual knowledge to a relationship with His Father. It is important that we do not miss that crucial point because that must also be our link. To Jesus, "being in My Father's house" was closely tied to learning about Him and loving Him. By asking questions about His Father, talking about Him, and listening to the teachers talk about Him and His law, He sought to know Him better. To Jesus, the pursuit of intellectual knowledge about God had nothing to do with wanting to appear smart in front of the teachers or gain favor. Instead, His desire to grow in the knowledge of God was inseparably linked to becoming more intimate with His Father.

As Christians, our attainment of knowledge should always have a personal aspect of intensifying our relationship with God. As a matter of fact, in John 15:15, Jesus alludes to the causal relationship between the degree of our closeness to Him and the amount of knowledge we have of Him. He says, "No longer do I call you slaves, for the slave does not know what His master is doing." In other words, we can be obedient to

His law (which is good), but we will still basically just follow orders and remain at the status of slaves. "But I have called you friends, for all things that I have heard from My Father I have made known to you." Stated differently, our closeness or status in our relationship with God increases with our knowledge about Him. Therefore, the more Jesus disclosed to His disciples about Himself and God, the closer and deeper the relationships became. Likewise, the more we seek to know God and His ways, the closer we will become to Him.

By harnessing our search for knowledge, we too can deepen our walk with God. By asking the right questions, the deep questions, we can learn more about God and profoundly improve our relationship with Him. And so, when we seek to grow in knowledge or when we seek to attain information about the world, our ultimate goal is not simply to learn about the world but rather to learn about the Creator of the world. Keep in mind, that when we talk about harnessing our search for knowledge we are not speaking about limits since God has no limits. Instead, we are talking about focusing on the things that will encourage the work of God in us and not things that will harm us.

My wife and I followed several "policies" when we were raising our sons. Some of those policies we created, some we adopted. One of our adopted policies involved dating. Our sons were not allowed to single date until they were sixteen. That is the way it was for my wife and her brothers as they were growing up and that is the way we decided it needed to be for our three sons. Recently, Becky's brother, Mark Beeson, a pastor with a beautiful 16-year-old daughter, sent me this e-mail message:

> In light of my daughter's recent interest in boys, I have been working on some means of screening potential candidates for dates—that she might actually begin to date, at some future time, maybe. This is a

working document. Any insights, additions, or helpful observations of improving this application form will be deeply appreciated.

Application for Permission to Date My Daughter

This application will be considered incomplete and rejected unless accompanied by an income statement, job history, and current medical report from your doctor.

NAME_____ DOB_____ IQ_____ GPA_____

BOY SCOUT RANK _____ CHURCH_____

• Do you have one male and one female parent? If not, please explain:

• The number of years your parents have been married:

• The best time to interview your father:

• The best time to interview your mother:

• The best time to interview your minister:

• Do you have a van? Yes No

• Do you own a truck with oversized tires? Yes No

• Do you own a waterbed? Yes No

• Do you have an earring, nose ring, belly button ring? Yes No

• Do you have a tattoo? Yes No

If you answered "yes" to any of the last five questions, discontinue the application and leave.

• In 25 words or less, what does this mean to you?
"Don't touch my daughter."

• In 25 words or less, what does "late" mean to you?

• Write a brief essay on "abstinence."

• What do you want to be if you grow up?

Please answer the following by completing each sentence:

• The one thing I hope this application does not ask me about is:

• A woman's place is in _____ .

• When I meet a girl the first thing I notice about her is
_____ .

I, _____ , hereby swear that all the above information is correct to the best of my knowledge, under the penalty of death, electrocution, Chinese water torture, etc.

Thank you for your interest! Please allow four to eight weeks for processing.

Don't call us—we'll call you!

My brother-in-law now insists that he only forwarded what had been anonymously sent to him. He continues to try, unsuccessfully, to pass this application off as something he was kidding about but we all know better. As you can see, the information that he wants on the application is meant to give him confidence in his daughter's date. The more he knows about the boy who is asking his daughter out on a date, the more comfortable he may feel with his taking her out. Likewise, the more we learn about God, the more knowledge we gain about His character and His ways, the more confidence we will have in Him.

As I have already mentioned, we have limitations in our abilities to understand God. We are also limited in our understanding of the world and of ourselves. As a people and as individuals we will always fall short of true understanding. That is why God admonished us to "Trust in the LORD with all your heart, and do not lean on your own understanding. In all your ways, acknowledge Him..." (Proverbs 3:5-6a). Our own intellectual abilities will never be sufficient for what we are going to need. Sure, we can acquire enough information to apply the formulas, but God does not want us to simply go through the mechanics of life. He wants us to acknowledge Him in all our ways. When we encounter problems and trials we might say something like, "I'm going through a hard time right now, and the outcome doesn't look good, but I know that You're with me and You have complete understanding of all my ways." He wants us to acknowledge His presence even when we fail to see Him or understand Him.

Proverbs 3:6 ends with, "and He will make your paths straight." He will make our paths straight—straight to Him. Eventually, we will find God in the circumstance or the problem when we yield to Him and seek Him. By trusting in God, getting to know Him and drawing nearer to Him, our lives will become more focused and more abundant.

Years ago, a friend in seminary told one of the best stories I have ever heard and it speaks to this point:

In a tiny German village there lived a young boy who had finally reached an age at which his mother would allow him to go into town by himself. He was very excited about this wonderful new opportunity and ran nearly all the way to the village. Relishing his independence, he caught his breath and strolled down the narrow streets.

The merchants going about their business fascinated him. At one point he stopped and stared as the breads were placed in the windows of the bakery. Then, at the shop next to the bakery, he watched intently as the freshly formed, wonderfully fragrant soaps were placed in their proper bins.

Soon he moved across the street and noticed through a big window a woodcarver busy with his craft. He watched that talented artist work—large slivers were carefully shaved from the huge piece of wood. As portions fell away, it appeared that he was making an elephant. The trunk and big ears were fairly obvious. The boy tapped on the window, gestured to the woodcarver and shouted, "It's an elephant!"

The woodcarver shook his head, smiled and then sliced off the ears.... sliced off the trunk, and continued carving. The little boy was intrigued. How could he have made a wrong guess? It had looked so much like an elephant that he could not believe he missed what was really being created.

Deciding to get a better view, he went into the shop. The woodcarver invited the boy to sit with him and a conversation ensued. "How old are you?" ...

"Do you have grandkids?"...

"What is your favorite subject in school?"...

"Do you like having white hair?"...

"How far away do you live?"...

As they chatted the old woodcarver continued whittling. A slender long neck and four legs became apparent. So, the boy with confidence stated, "I know what it is now. It's a giraffe!"

Off came the neck, and legs were whittled into splinters.

The boy was slightly irritated, because he was just sure it was a giraffe. However, he was enthralled with the conversation, so he stayed.

"Have you always carved wood?"...

"Why did you come into the village today?"...

As they talked, the woodcarver continued to work. Beautiful wings and an S-curved neck made it clear that a swan was soon to be present in the room. "I know what you are making. It is a swan!"

The woodcarver quickly whittled away the wings and neck.

The boy became very frustrated. The conversation was no longer the primary reason he was staying there. He was going to find out what it was that the woodcarver was making. With the tiny piece of wood that remained, that should be evident very soon.

The boy watched intently as the wood carver whittled. And whittled. And whittled. Finally, nothing at all was left in the hands of the woodcarver. A pile of shavings lay on the floor.

The boy was furious! "I stayed here with you all this time and you weren't making anything!"

The woodcarver stood up, put his hand on the boy's shoulder, looked him straight in the eye and said, "Oh, but I was! I was making time for us to talk and get to know each other!"

That story makes well the point that it takes time together to build a relationship. How can we relate to God? The same way we relate with each other. We can spend time with Him. We can acknowledge and value His presence in our lives by sharing our perspectives, fears, and joys. We can actively seek to experience Him in the everyday activities of our lives through our spouses, children, family, and friends. By reading the Bible and praying, we can learn about Him and allow His Spirit to teach us and change us. We can experience His love through other Christians and through worshiping God with them regularly. Just as we would pursue any valuable relationship, in the same way we can pursue Christ. Relating to Him through the knowledge He gives us, our lives can truly be changed.

As we set out to actively commit to God, obey His commands, and pursue true knowledge, we can take comfort in the fact that He is the One who guides us through the entire relationship.

Never will He leave us. Though we may face struggles on the path toward the holiness of God, He is always nearby to hold us up and comfort us. Even when we resist Him by being foolish, prideful, evasive, and hateful, it is relieving to know that Jesus consistently approaches us in forgiveness and restoration. He always comes to us in love, never in condemnation. In fact, He often changes us before we are aware of His presence. Like children in the care of their parents, we are constantly being guided by His hands. As we try to love, He simply walks alongside us and brings up things He wants to do with us. He wants us to fall more deeply in love with Him.

In the next chapter, we discover how to take action as we surrender to holiness in prayer. Additionally, we get a glimpse of the significance of the unity of believers. Through prayer God intensifies and sharpens our focus. As growing Christians, prayer is the most essential element in our lives because it is our direct link to our Father. We can see how faithful He is when we pray. By praying expectantly and purposefully, our lives can be transformed. Through unity with other Christians, God offers His Spirit, character, and power in flesh and blood. By relying on the gentle strength of God, we see the importance of relationships in our lives and begin to explore the unique and challenging ways He calls us to respond to others. God's ways are mysterious. The world might even say that they are peculiar, but discovering them is both freeing and exciting.

Peculiarities
of Holiness

"The holy is above all aesthetic as well as moral and logical classifications—it is the 'wholly other' transcending all worldly values."

—*I. Maybaum, Synagogue and Society*

CHAPTER THREE

*T*he good news about holiness is that through the new life we have in Jesus Christ, God provides us with a way to holiness. Holiness is not something we grasp on our own by trying harder, learning more, or being better. Just as we cannot save ourselves, neither can we make ourselves holy. We must come to an acute awareness that God alone has forged the pathway for us and our role in the process involves choosing the path He set before us even when it may seem quite strange to the world.

Plato, a Greek philosopher in the fourth century BC, believed that life could be viewed from two perspectives: the sensible and the intelligible. According to Plato, most of us believe only in one type of reality—sensible reality. It is experienced through our physical senses—seeing, hearing, touching, smelling, or tasting. Thoughts, ideas, and beliefs not experienced in the material world—intelligible reality—are deemed nonexistent or unimportant.

In *The Republic,* Plato created an allegory for his theory by describing a group of individuals trapped inside a large cave.

Their view of life, then, was confined to what they could experience within the cave. Trapped since birth and never able to comprehend that there could be anything beyond their situation, even flickering shadows on the walls were real and significant. Then one day someone ventured out of the cave, encountered the light of day, and began to recognize the stark difference between the illusions of the cave and the truth of life outside.

The cave symbolizes the material world in which we live (sensible reality). It is a world we experience through our physical senses. Plato thought that believing only in that kind of reality welcomes ignorance. On the other hand, the outside of the cave, which he used to represent all that we fail to experience or welcome into our existence—intelligible reality—is a world of ideas and revelation. Plato thought that those of us who are wise acquire true knowledge and understanding by sharpening our intelligible view of reality. Perceiving the world through ideas, inner meditation, and theories helps to set us free from the prison of ignorance, so by choosing to exist only in a sensible reality we foolishly trap ourselves. We live behind the walls of our own ignorance by refusing to allow the light of knowledge to free us.

Centuries after Plato, in the mid-1600s, Thomas Hobbs used some of Plato's theory to write his book *Leviathan*. Hobbs basically agreed with Plato that most of us do not truly believe in anything else beyond the cave (sensible reality). He went on to add that since the majority of us believe in nothing else beyond human existence and since all of us have a strong desire for peace, the only solution to the world's problems is for us to surrender to an ultimate power within the world. In other words, the only way we can achieve order in the world is by totally submitting to a powerful human leader or leaders.

Sadly, that is exactly the same type of philosophy used to promote Nazism.

Fortunately there is another view unlike that of Hobbs. It places little faith in our endeavors and recognizes the limitations that exist from a human-centered perspective. Though similar to Plato's belief in intelligible reality, it involves much more than the stoic pursuit of ideas through inner meditation; it says we need to be trained to listen "beyond the cave"—beyond our common perceptions of reality. But such training is a formidable challenge, especially when we are trying to learn to hear from God.

Even the prophet Samuel had some difficulty recognizing God's voice. While sleeping in the temple, he heard a voice speak to him (1 Samuel 3). Since Samuel was under the care of Eli, the high priest, and was accustomed to hearing his voice, he ran to Eli and said, "Here I am, for you called me." But Eli said, "No, I did not" and told him to go back to sleep. As with most people, Samuel had become so acquainted with things inside the cave, that he never considered the call could have originated from the LORD. He did not recognize the voice of God. Finally, after God had called him for the third time, Eli recognized what was happening.

> Then Eli discerned that the LORD was calling the boy. And Eli said to Samuel, "Go lie down, and it shall be if He calls you, that you shall say, 'Speak, LORD, for Thy servant is listening.'"
> (I Samuel 3:8b9)

By training his ears to hear God, Samuel began to yield to God and eventually became a faithful prophet to his people.

Hearing the voice of God is a matter of listening beyond our surroundings and beyond the familiar. It involves listening beyond our preconceptions, worries, and agendas. In order to hear Him, we must have the correct reference point, which is not inside the cave.

Like Samuel, we must actively seek ways to commune with God if we truly desire to know Him. However, as we have already discussed, holiness means set apart for God's work. So it follows that our ways of pursuing God will be strange to the world.

> *Hearing the voice of God is a matter of listening beyond our surroundings and beyond the familiar. It involves listening beyond our preconceptions, worries, and agendas. In order to hear Him, we must have the correct reference point.*

Following the pathway to holiness is not about doing things to find Him. People of many religions tend to concentrate on doing things for their gods—doing prayers, doing sacrifices, doing acts of service, doing rituals, doing traditions, etc. These things are perceived as pathways to their gods.

Perhaps the most unique, separate, and distinct aspect of our relationship with God is the way He uses prayer. Instead of prayer being something we are supposed to do, God sees it as something we are. He wants our lives to become prayers to

Him and practicing prayer is the beginning of this. Yet to "cave dwellers," prayer is foolish and worthless and we, too, have been bathed in such ideology. To us, it is peculiar and frightening to trust in something outside the cave (outside of our experience). At times, we may believe:

- Prayer is a waste of time.

- We can accomplish more through action than through prayer.

- God already knows what we need—so it is not necessary to pray.

- Prayer is simply a "feel good" psychological exercise.

The fact is, if we desire to seek holiness through a deep relationship with God, we begin with prayer. We start by asking God to help. Prayer requires trusting in Someone else, being vulnerable, relying on that which is unseen, and waiting patiently. It grates hard against many of our natural, sinful tendencies. To most of the world, prayer seems strange.

As we explore the pathway to holiness we will discover that prayer is more than laying our requests before Him. It involves getting to know Him. It also involves God revealing to us who we are to Him. By praying continually and expectantly we come to see His character reflected in our own. We begin to see what is valuable in our lives and what is holding us back. If we are to do anything significant with our lives we must have focus and that comes through prayer. Prayer is our primary venue to holiness.

Before We Pray

On the fifteenth of May, in the Jungle of Nool,
In the heat of the day, in the cool of the pool,

> He was splashing . . . enjoying the jungle's great joys . . .
> When Horton the elephant heard a small noise.

In the classic children's book, *Horton Hears a Who,* by Dr. Seuss, the kind-hearted elephant believes there is a community of small creatures living on a speck of dust. He swears to his jungle friends that he can hear them speaking to him. Yet no matter how hard he tries, he cannot convince them of the truth. They laugh at him, tease him, and even attempt to cage him because they think he is a fool—until they finally hear the voice of the "whos." We may not encounter that kind of opposition when we talk to our God who is unseen, but we will experience considerable resistance from the world and from inside ourselves. Even though prayer appears to be a simple act of talking to God and listening to His voice, it is amazing how skillfully we resist the call to be still before Him.

A relationship with God goes beyond His response to our prayers. It encompasses our reverence and love for Him.

When we are praying, sometimes we can feel like we are merely speaking to the walls or the small specks of dust floating by us in the air. We are not! Like the rest of our Christian walk, prayer is rooted in faith. In this fast-paced world, possessing steady faith in anything is a considerable challenge to us in and of itself. We do not like waiting when there is so much to do. We are so accustomed to getting immediate responses to our requests that we expect God's response to our prayers to be like our ATM cards: fast and accurate. The truth is that a relationship with God goes beyond His response to our prayers. It encompasses our reverence and love for Him.

Consider the words of Jesus after his resurrection, when He spoke to Thomas: "Because you have seen Me, you have believed. Blessed are they who did not see, and yet believed" (John 20:29). According to Jesus, as we respond to God in faith we will experience His blessings even when we do not hear or see Him. In a way, not seeing or hearing Jesus while we pray blesses us more than if we saw Him as Thomas did. Believing in God who is unseen both presupposes and strengthens faith. Think about this: even Jesus, who is God the Son, rarely experienced what we would perceive to be earth-shattering prayer sessions during His time on earth— except for the transfiguration (Matthew 17). Instead, His prayers were rooted in His intimacy with the Father. That is, He believed in God the Father and knew that He was heard. By becoming sensitive to His Father's inaudible voice, He was inexplicably able to hear Him. We, as well, are being faithful when we pray to God, although we may not perceive an immediate reward in it. The fact that God loves, blesses, and tests us through prayer is brought to light through the following story about a father who had a delightful relationship with his daughter. He absolutely adored his girl. They had always spent lots of time together—going to the mall, doing yard work, and playing games. However, around Christmas time, his then 10-year-old girl started distancing herself from him. Instead of accepting his invitations to go to the mall, she would say, "Dad, you go to the mall. I really need to stay here." When he would invite her to join him on an evening walk, she would say, "Umm, sorry Dad, but I just want to be alone in my room right now."

The father really started to feel badly. In fact, he was very hurt and wondered what was happening to their relationship. Finally, Christmas day came and the father opened one of the gifts his daughter had wrapped for him. Inside the box was a pair of slippers. She had learned how to make them at a Girl Scouts' meeting.

She smiled at him and said, "Dad, this is what I have been doing the whole time. What do you think?"

The father looked at her and said, "Honey, I love these slippers, and I love the fact that you love me enough to make them." He hugged her warmly. "But do me a favor. Next time, let's buy the slippers and spend time together, because that is what's important to me. And that is what I have missed so much."

God feels that way about us, too. He longs more for the times we spend with Him than for the things we do for Him. Prayer is an act of intimacy. He loves it when we trust in His unseen presence and kneel before Him in faith. We do not need to beg for Him to help us or give to us. He loves us whether or not we pray. He will always care for us. He will always love us.

When we pray, how much of the time is spent in praise and in building a relationship with God? How much of our prayer time is merely requests? While God expects us to tell Him our needs and request His help, we must also prepare our hearts to draw near to Him.

Praying to Discover

A.W. Tozer once said that you could predict a man's reaction to God based on "his concept of who God is, because subconsciously that man will either run to or run from that concept." Our concept of God profoundly effects our response to Him—in prayer, in action, and in faith. In order to hear from God we not only require the correct reference point (prayer), but we also need the correct vision of God and ourselves. We need to view God for who He is and not for how He fits in with us. In addition, we must strive to see one another as God sees us.

> *We must strive to see one another as God sees us.*

Upon believing in Jesus Christ as our LORD and Savior some amazing things take place. Not only are we pardoned from our sins and given eternal life, but also God unduly blesses us. He blesses us in heaven, on earth, and from within:

> Blessed be the God and Father of our LORD Jesus Christ, who has blessed us with every spiritual blessing in the heavenly places in Christ. (Ephesians 1:3)

> Seeing that His divine power has granted to us everything pertaining to life and godliness, through the true knowledge of Him who called us by His own glory and excellence. For by these He has granted to us His precious and magnificent promises ... (II Peter 1:3-4a)

The Bible states that we are being blessed with "every spiritual blessing" and are being endowed with "His precious and magnificent promises." Those are facts, not empty promises.

Every promise God makes He keeps. And we more fully realize His blessings as we really believe Him and act accordingly.

> *Hopefully, God is showing through each one of us who have asked Him to come into our lives as our personal LORD and Savior.*

Not too long ago I heard a cute story about a little girl who, on the way home from church, turned to her mother and said, "Mommy, the preacher's sermon this morning confused me."

The mother said, "Oh! Why is that?"

The girl replied, "Well, he said that God is bigger than we are. Is that true?"

"Yes, that's true," the mother replied.

"He also said that God lives within us. Is that true, too?"

Again the mother replied, "Yes."

"Well," said the girl. "If God is bigger than us and He lives in us, wouldn't He show through?"

Hopefully, God is showing through each one of us who have asked Him to come into our lives as our personal LORD and Savior. It is through prayer that we acknowledge His divine presence in our lives. As we pray, we openly recognize our inadequacy and His supremacy. Then God helps us discover those things in our lives that we need to give to Him. As we mature in our connection with God, He will begin to consume those parts of us that need to die. Eventually God's holiness will remove the moral decay from our being.

A while ago, I read a scientific article that provided me with a graphic analogy of how God works in our lives. It involved the use of maggots in surgery. Apparently, during the Civil War, maggots were used in the healing of certain types of open wounds. They were called "surgical maggots." Recently, the medical community has begun utilizing them again. The fascinating aspect about these kinds of maggots is that they will only eat dead or decaying flesh. They do not damage healthy flesh. So, for certain kinds of wounds, hospitals are purchasing clean maggots to put on sores that have become resistant to antibiotics. When placed on the wounds, the maggots do their work by devouring any dead flesh. Once all of the dead flesh has been consumed the maggots are removed.

Even though it is a rather revolting depiction, it provides us with a striking illustration of what holiness does within us. In time, God somehow consumes those parts of us that are dead and rotting away. He removes those sins from our hearts that could destroy us, so we may think of prayer as an invitation to God to perform surgery. While He is doing the work, He does not leave us unaware. In fact, God helps us to discover what He is doing in our lives. Through prayer, God involves us in His plan.

Praying Continually

Bobby Knight, a coach of the Indiana Hoosiers basketball team, was once interviewed on *60 Minutes* and was asked, "What does it take to be a team that's continually in the top rankings and continually winning?" Before the coach could respond however, the interviewer interjected, "It must certainly take the will to win."

Bobby Knight replied, "It does. It takes the will to win. However, it primarily takes something even more important than that—it takes the will to prepare. It takes the will to go out every day and practice the fundamentals over and over until they become second nature, and then first nature to you."

Even though prayer is not basketball, the well-made point is transferable. By drilling the fundamentals of prayer into our daily routine prayer can become second nature, even first nature to us. The Bible admonishes us to "Seek the LORD and His strength; seek His face continually" (1 Chronicles 16:11). How do we get to the place where we are seeking His face continually? And Paul instructed us to "Pray without ceasing" (1 Thessalonians 5:17). Now how in the world do we do that? The answer to both of those questions is that we do it in God's strength. While it begins with some effort on our part it should ultimately depend upon God.

Considering Jesus again, was there ever a time when He was not in communion with His Father? Was there ever a time when He was on His own and without God's guidance? I do not believe so. Even as He hung on the cross and cried out "My God, my God, why hast Thou forsaken me?" He was reciting from Psalm 22:1 as it predicted the suffering Messiah. Jesus' life was a constant and continual prayer to the Father.

The exciting news is that prayer can become an integral part of our lives. We, too, can have that kind of closeness with God. Our lives can be prayers to Him. Our lives can be so absorbed with God that we will experience loneliness and pain when we shift our focus away from Him. Yet not very many of us pray continually as Jesus did. We are often too occupied with our everyday activities to pray.

Jesus said, "No servant can serve two masters. Either he will hate the one and love the other, or he will be devoted to the one and despise the other" (Luke 16:13 NIV). So, either we are seeking and serving God throughout our day or we are serving another power; we cannot serve both.

We can fill our lives with prayer if we envision what we do every day in ways that remind us of God. For instance, some of us are builders of homes, of people, or of structures. God is a builder. Some of us are healers of physical, psychological, or spiritual problems. God is a healer. Some of us are leaders, encouragers, teachers, faithful servants, students, parents, children, judges, lawmakers, or law enforcers. God is or has been all of these.

Another way we can experience prayer-full lives is by fasting. Jesus practiced fasting even though He was perfect. Many of the founding church fathers practiced fasting. Fasting is a way of putting behind, just briefly, the daily responsibilities that fill our lives so that we can realize the greatest offer that has ever been made: God's love. Fasting is an important practice in our Christian walk because most of us have become reasonably successful at satisfying ourselves with the things of the world. We know how to create comfortable environments and to make things convenient for ourselves. However, something unintentional happens to us in the midst of that process. Instead of relying on God for our satisfaction we begin to rely on the world.

In Deuteronomy 8, the LORD instructed the Israelites to be careful to obey His commands and walk in His ways. He admonished them to remember that He was the One who rescued them from slavery, brought them safely through the wilderness, and provided for them. When they had eaten and were satisfied, He encouraged and welcomed their praises to

Him. He also warned them that if they began to believe that the power and the strength of their own hands had provided this wealth for them and if they began to honor other gods, they would perish (Deuteronomy 8:17b-19).

Fasting is an important practice in our Christian walk, because most of us have become reasonably successful at satisfying ourselves with the things of the world.

In a manner of speaking, we are no different than the Israelites. We have structured our lives so as to get more and more from them—more comfort, more security, and more wealth. While it is certainly understandable, the spiritual effect on our lives is devastating. Instead of allowing God to bless us with His comfort, security, and treasures, we end up seeking immediate gratification through the world. We become so bound by the tempting offers of the world that we are unable to pull ourselves away to experience God's blessings. The pleasures of the world become driving needs rather than occasional creature comforts. The securities of the world appear to become absolute necessities. Ultimately, the things that gave us satisfaction become the things that keep us from real satisfaction.

A Fast Fix

The primary reason for fasting is to teach us to rely on God and to value what is eternal. It forces our bodies and hearts to depend upon Him. It also demonstrates a sobering truth: that we do not need the world as desperately as we need God.

When we fast we are not simply getting rid of the things of the flesh. Fasting primarily entails substituting satisfaction offered by the world for the satisfaction of God. We not only need to put to death the works and desires of the flesh, but we also must seize the things of the Spirit and endeavor to discover what truly pleases God. Through fasting, our pain is transformed into prayers to Him. Experiencing the pain of denying our flesh draws us closer into relationship with God.

> *Ultimately, the things that gave us satisfaction become the things that keep us from real satisfaction.*

As it takes time to grow in maturity as a Christian, it likewise takes time to learn how to fast, how to pray, and how to hear God. We can, though, take steps that bring us closer to that maturity. We can set aside a day, a week, or even longer to fast. While we fast our prayers and communion with God fill the empty times. When it comes to choosing something from which to fast, there are four categories:

The first category is fasting from striving. God said, "Be still, and know that I am God" (Psalm 46:10a NIV). The translation in the New American Standard Bible says it another way: "Cease striving." He issues that command because He loves us and wants us to hear from Him. It is not because He thinks what we do has no value, it is just that He knows our tendencies to fill our lives with excitement, accomplishments, and possessions so as to forget our sorrows, worries, and frustrations. Being still before God means turning to Him to be made content.

Most of us occupy even our spare moments with striving. What if, instead, we fill them with prayer? Then we can continue to get to know God better and experience the blessings of that. This does not have to be a difficult or complicated process.

For example, as we drive, we can fast from the noise of the radio. In the silence, we can pray for the people we know or for the people in the cars around us. We do not have to know their specific needs. God already knows what those are and our prayers for others will be effective. Another way (and there are many) to stay close to Him, is to recall a past sermon or testimony, a good point from a book, or a Scripture passage.

The second category is fasting from habits. This is a tough one because habits comfort us, at least partially, by the familiarity of the routines themselves. We can, though, purpose to fast from habits that are not building our relationship with God.

For example, some of us when we are down or confused are in the habit of relying solely on a specific person instead of on God for encouragement and support. We need to make sure we are not isolated from the input of godly people, but always depending on a specific person's solution or encouragement can actually distract us from experiencing God's full blessing. We can choose to go to God for help the next time that we feel unsettled.

Others of us are so involved with a small circle of friends that we have unwittingly shut many people out of our lives. Breaking out of our routines and hearing what God is doing in the lives of others is also a way of fasting from our predictable behaviors. Something as simple as choosing a new place to sit in church can help us get a new perspective on more than just the pulpit.

The third category is fasting from certain types of substances in our lives. The most common of all substance fasts is the fast from food. However, some other substances to consider fasting from are nicotine, caffeine, alcohol, or other select pleasures that over time become addictions to us. While drugs provide temporary emotional comfort by dulling our senses and lessening current stresses or pains, they do not offer real hope and recovery. We use substances in an attempt to fill needs that can only be filled by God. Running to cigarettes, beer, or coffee for comfort is never the perfect solution. We need to figure out what it is we are really looking for and ask God to lead us toward that. God will help us and we will realize how useless a substance is in answering our needs. We will find ourselves praying a lot more and depending on Him for comfort. Fasting and praying to God will allow Him to help us work through the pain instead of numbing it or running from it.

The last category involves fasting from impulsive emotions. Many of us have specific emotions that we return to when things get tough. For some of us, the answer is to worry. We worry about the future. We worry about the past. We worry about our safety. We worry about others. There is no end to the things that cause us to worry. Jesus knew that when He said, "Therefore do not be anxious for tomorrow; for tomorrow will care for itself. Each day has enough trouble of its own" (Matthew 6:34). Worrying is usually about trying to gain control over things that are beyond our control. When we worry, we fail to trust in God. Like Peter who feared the wind and rain when he walked on the water toward Jesus, we let the storms around us fill us with fear and cause us to sink into despair (Matthew 14: 22–33).

Those of us who are worriers can choose to fast from worrying for just one day at a time. Instead of worrying we can say, "God, I trust You with this. Instead of worrying right now, I will believe that You are good and that You will intervene. I choose to trust You instead of trusting worry."

Worrying is usually about trying to gain control over things that are beyond our control. When we worry, we fail to trust in God.

Another impulsive emotion is anger. Many of us have anger issues that have progressed unresolved for years. In fact, we sometimes use anger to drive us. It gives us energy. Anger, however, is a destroyer when it is ungodly. By fasting, we can take a couple of days and say, "God, I am going to fast from anger. I am not going to be angry with anybody because You said, 'Vengeance is Mine.' Instead of becoming angry, I am going to let You have the control. I am not going to try to control the issue with my anger."

The final impulsive emotion is very common and powerful. It is self-pity. With it, we experience a range of feelings— remorse, shame, sadness, despair, and hopelessness. Some of us are caught in a cycle. Our thoughts seem to continually focus on our own sadness and victimization. For some of us, self-pity can lead to depression. Instead of allowing our emotions to take over, we could determine to spend the whole day in praise to God for what He has given us and for what He has already done in our hearts. Choosing to fast from the emotion of self-pity can force incredible dependence on God. Contact with God and His goodness can transform a lonely heart in a short time. Fasting from our predictable emotions permits God to take control and helps us to see the benefits of His intervention in our lives.

It is important to mention that when self-pity does lead to depression that can certainly be more that "just a mood." Some types of depression may need to be resolved through prayer accompanied by either counseling or medication. When it comes to major depression, seeking help from a professional is necessary.

Praying Expectantly

Years ago, there was an old church located in a rural region of the western prairies. During what was typically the rainy season, there had been a tremendous drought. For months it had barely rained at all. The farmers and sharecroppers in the area suffered greatly because their crops had begun to wither and die. Eventually, the idea spread throughout the community to pray for rain. Everyone grew excited about the possibility of God answering their prayers and decided upon an appointed day to come together at the church to pray. As the people crowded their way into the small church, they talked amongst themselves and waited restlessly for the preacher to begin the meeting. When he arrived at the pulpit, he stood silently while surveying the people before him. Then he said, "Brothers and sisters, you know why we're here today. You know we came to pray. Before we begin, I've got just one question for you." He paused, making sure he had everyone's attention. "Where are your umbrellas?"

Praying expectantly demands that we act accordingly because He who promised is faithful.

When we pray to God for something, we need to act as if we are going to receive it. Praying expectantly demands that we act accordingly because He who promised is faithful. Jesus said, "Therefore I tell you, whatever you ask for in prayer, believe that you have received it, and it will be yours" (Mark 11:24). If we want new jobs, then praying expectantly demands that we keep our eyes open for the opportunities that God will bring to us. If we desire to be more patient with our children, then praying expectantly demands that we seek ways to practice patience in our daily routines. If we long for a relationship to be restored, then praying expectantly demands that we prepare our hearts for that time and take the necessary steps toward restoration. God will always answer our prayers, but it is our job to believe that He hears them. Acting on our belief proves our faith in Him.

When God said to Noah, "I am going to bring floodwaters on the earth to destroy all life…" (Genesis 6:17a, NIV) Noah did not think to himself, "Well, I'm just gonna wait 'til I see the rain before I prepare." Instead, he started preparing. He acted. In fact, it took 120 years for him to complete the ark!

When God said to Abram, "I am going to make you into a great nation,"(Genesis12:2a, NIV) Abram did not respond by standing still and living his life as he previously had. Instead, he walked out into the desert to follow God. His body acted in faith before he ever saw the first glimpse of the promise fulfilled.

When we pray for something, how ready are we to act on that prayer? Are we prepared to receive the answer when God delivers it?

> ## *The exciting and liberating truth is that we have Jesus as our example and Savior.*

When the LORD commanded the Israelites to take possession of the land of Canaan in Numbers 13 and 14, He was answering their prayers. If they had obeyed His command, their trek to the Promised Land would have been short and they would have enjoyed a land flowing with milk and honey. Instead, they feared the men of Canaan and disobeyed God. Although God had willingly blessed them throughout their journey in the desert, the Israelites failed to practice their faith in Him. Instead of acting on their prayers by trusting God, they used prayers to get what they wanted from Him. Thus, because of their failure to act in faith they were condemned to wander in the desert for forty years.

The Israelites' experience can help us recognize our own propensity to mistrust God even when He has proven otherwise. Thankfully, we have a written account of God's work in the lives of His chosen people. With the Bible, we can observe the examples of God's faithfulness in Scripture and therefore grow in faith vicariously. That historical record is a confirmation beyond what we have seen Him do in our own lives. The exciting and liberating truth is that we have Jesus as our example and Savior. Several times throughout the New Testament, Jesus instructed us how to pray and encouraged us with the faithfulness of His Father. For that reason, Chapter 5 of this book will focus even more specifically on how to pray. In Matthew 7:7-11, Jesus said to His disciples:

> Ask, and it shall be given to you; seek, and you shall find; knock, and it shall be opened to you. For everyone who asks receives, and he who seeks finds, and to him who knocks it shall be opened. Or what man is there among you, when his son shall ask him for a loaf, will give him a stone? Or if he shall ask for a fish, he will not give him a snake, will he? If you then, being evil, know how to give good gifts to your children, how much more shall your Father who is in heaven give what is good to those who ask Him!

When we explore the meaning, verb tense, and mood behind the words in this passage they reveal some amazing truths. For instance, the word "ask" is written in the present tense. This connotes a continual and repetitive action. So Jesus told us to ask again and again and again. We have the freedom to approach God with anything. God wants us to keep asking, to keep requesting, and to keep calling upon Him. In addition, the word "ask" is written in the imperative mood. In other words, God commanded us to pray. When we feel like praying it is God who is moving in us. We never come into prayer by our own authority. Prayer is not our idea. God calls us into prayer by the movement of His Holy Spirit and we respond accordingly by asking, seeking, and knocking. So what does that mean for us? It means that when we feel like praying, God is working and we need to respond to His call.

Since God bids us to pray, then it is not presumptuous for us to expect Him to answer. We should never hesitate to ask of God or expect His response. Our prayers are not a case of pleading or bargaining with God. He wants to hear from us. He wants to give to us. Praying expectantly, then, is not presumptuous but logical. Therefore, it is important to make sure that we order our lives so that we receive His answer. Because Jesus said, "Everyone who asks, receives," we know He is going to answer us. In addition to asking God for something, we are also commanded to seek and knock for it as well. Both seeking and knocking involve action. They exercise our faith and obedience by making us arrange our lives for His answer. While our prayer time and communion with God is crucial, an equally important time occurs afterwards when we must decide between action and inaction.

> *Because Jesus said, "Everyone who asks, receives," we know He is going to answer us.*

Like most people, we pray for something and then continue to build our lives on the basis of not getting it. Or maybe we pray about it for an extended period of time and then forget about it, hoping to be surprised by the answer sometime in the future. But God said, "Commit your way to the LORD" (Psalm 37:5a). He calls us to obedience in response to who He is and our relationship with Him.

Should those who are single and praying for "the love of your life" wait until that love appears before preparing? The answer to that question is no. Right now, as singles, practice working in cooperation with others. By practicing selflessness and sensitivity toward close friends and family, preparation for marriage begins even before mates have been met. Then when God reveals that special person, it will not be so much of an adjustment because of all the preparation.

When we are praying for good health, how are we trusting God in our prayers? If we have been sick for awhile, it is easy to settle into a perspective that sickness will be a part of our future. Instead, we need to seek to adopt a healthy outlook and make an effort to do just a little more each day than we feel like doing. Because, if we choose to make our illness an integral part of our identity we may miss the joy of God's blessing when He brings healing.

If we have been praying for financial freedom to get out of debt or at least be able to pay the bills, what choices are we making to live up to those prayers? A poor (in every sense of the word) choice is to continue charging everything to credit cards. When financial freedom seems like an unattainable goal, the non-solution of continued charging is likely to be our choice. Instead, we need to trust that God will give us what we need, day by day. Believing that God will provide and taking prudent corrective actions involves wise stewardship and faithful tithing on our part. To pray expectantly we can say, "God, I trust in You. I know You will give me what I need to live my life. I am going to glorify You through my financial faithfulness."

When we begin to live and behave as if our prayers will be answered, something wonderful starts to happen. Our lives become so in tune with God that we recognize His answer even when it is not what we expected. We learn to become satisfied and sensitized to God's responses to our prayers.

Although the Bible says that He is going to answer our prayers, it does not say how He will answer us. Nonetheless, by acting on our prayers, we respond to God's work in our lives even when we cannot see the end result. Our prayers will be answered based on His truth and goodness. All of the actions we take with our prayers should be sifted through God's Word.

Praying in Unity

The ideal starting point in our pursuit of holiness is prayer. To pray as an individual is great but there is something powerful and transforming about praying together with others. Jesus said:

> Again I say to you, that if two of you agree on earth about anything that they may ask, it shall be done for them by My Father who is in heaven. For where two or three have gathered together in my name, there I am in their midst. (Matthew 18:19-20)

Since our Christian life is not ultimately about personal improvement, neither is our path toward holiness. Jesus intended prayer to be both personal and communal. Ultimately, just as prayer links us to God, prayer will link us to each other. By praying together with purpose, praying for one another, and praying for specific needs, we are drawn closer by God's loving hand.

A recent Gallup survey found that the happiness of married couples was directly proportionate to how often they prayed together—even above the amount of sexual intimacy. This study was published in a secular magazine. Thus, the old adage, "The family that prays together, stays together," seems to stand firm. Obviously, there is something intimate and powerful about praying together. It binds us together as a family.

In heaven, we will all be united as a family. In fact, we are part of the family of God even now. We are not simply isolated and independent individuals. We are connected to each other in ways we probably will not understand until we reach heaven. God's ultimate desire for us is to be in unity. Before Jesus was taken to the cross, He prayed to His Father for the family of believers (John 17:21). He prayed that we would become one just as He and the Father are one. Holiness and maturity in Christ are not attributes we can pursue alone. Through prayer, God not only draws us and transforms us, but He unites us.

> *When we begin to live and behave as if our prayers will be answered, something wonderful starts to happen. Our lives become so in tune with God that we recognize His answer even when it is not what we expected.*

As we set foot on the pathway to holiness in prayer, we will grow more and more in knowledge and understanding of God's plan for our lives and for the lives of those around us. By praying continually, we can begin to break free from the shackles of the world and depend upon God's perfect blessings. As we pray expectantly and seek His answers, our actions will begin to line up with His plan for our lives. Finally, praying in unity will add power and purpose to our prayers. It can bring us closer to God's ultimate purpose for our lives, which is unity with Him and with each other.

In Chapter 5, we will continue on our journey down the peculiar path of prayer as we study the greatest prayer ever prayed, the LORD's Prayer. Jesus will walk us through how to pray to God and how to determine His will. However, we will discover some of the typical pruning patterns of God as we surrender to His will. Throughout our journey, God will persist in removing those things from our lives that could cause us harm. By recognizing them in our lives and allowing Him access to them, we can free ourselves from the needless pain and suffering that they could produce. In addition to the removal of that which is harmful, He will also begin to fill us with His winsome and mysterious qualities. They are attributes that will bring joy not only to us, but also to those around us.

Pruning
of Holiness

"Concerning Jesus' statement that 'Strait is the gate, and narrow is the way, which leadeth unto life, and few there be that find it: The big battalions will never be gathered before the narrow door. One of the real reasons why there are so few Christians is that Christianity is a very stern creed, a creed for heroes, while we are good-natured little people who wish to have a good time, and to give others a good time."

—*Dean Inge*

CHAPTER FOUR

A farmer stood watching his sheep graze in the pasture. A salesman approached and began talking with him. The old farmer, weathered and wise, barely acknowledged the salesman and just kept watching his sheep. Then, right in the middle of the salesman's pitch, he abruptly interrupted. "Excuse me, young man. I've got to do something."

Placing his fingers to his mouth, he whistled loudly. The salesman looked up. A dog that until then had been sitting mindlessly among the sheep sprang into action. Upon hearing the whistle, it rounded up the entire herd and ushered them toward the pen. Then, darting through the crowd of sheep, the dog released the latch with its paw and shoved the gate open with its nose. Racing back to the rear of the herd, it guided all of the sheep into the pen, shut the gate, and latched it with its paw.

The salesman was amazed. "I've never seen anything like that in my life!"

"Yep!" The farmer acknowledged. "Taught him everything he knows. Took me a long time, but I did it."

The salesman remarked, "That is absolutely phenomenal! What is the dog's name?"

A perplexed expression came over the farmer's face. "Name?" he asked. "What's his name?" They both stood silently for a long time while the farmer tried to remember the name. Suddenly, he smiled and turned to the salesman. "What's the name of that flower that is red, good smellin,' and has a long stem—with thorns on it?"

The salesman answered, "Rose?"

Nodding, the farmer said, "Yeah, that's it!" He then turned to his wife who was standing on the front porch. "Hey Rose, what do we call that dog?"

Obviously, the farmer had neglected something in the training of his dog. Certainly, he had accomplished a great deal. He taught the dog to wait patiently in the pasture, to respond to his call, to herd the sheep toward the pen, to unlatch and open the gate, and to close and latch the gate. Yet, he had also lost something in the process. Inadvertently, he neglected what Jesus would call the weightier or more important issues. Focusing intently on training the dog, the farmer failed to get to know its name. Not only could he not remember the dog's name, but he had also forgotten his wife's name! While it is an entertaining story, it also demonstrates our tendency to sacrifice the intimate and personal aspects of our lives for the urgent and sometimes superficial.

Pursuing holiness in our own strength and with our own agenda is nothing more than works-based religion and human effort. Reading through this chapter, sifting through the relevant information, and applying the principles to our lives will not guarantee intimacy with God or holiness. Life changing transformation begins and ends with our closeness to God. Our actions should be motivated by our closeness, because holiness is not about behavior; rather it is about intimacy.

As a part of our intimacy with Him, God's holiness sets us free from materials and people that tempt or entice us. He also releases us from anger, a vengeful spirit, and lust. Our inclination to eliminate our sins and acquire the fruits of the Spirit on our own results from our desire to be in control. We love the feelings of pride, significance, and security that control gives us, especially when we accomplish something.

So, we need to consider whether or not we are on the right track toward holiness. Are we doing this in our own strength, with our own goals, and on our own timetable? Are we "being still" and truly worshiping Him, or are we trying to gain control again? Unless we purposely test ourselves and allow God to search our hearts throughout the process of holiness (2 Corinthians 13:5), we will simply trudge through the routine and neglect what is truly important. Unless we recognize that God is the One who works in us to will and act according to His good purpose (Philippians 2:13), we will believe that our victories and successes are rooted in our achievements, our hard work, and our character.

It cannot be stressed enough that God is the One who draws and changes us. Jesus said in John 6:44a, "No one can come to Me, unless the Father who sent Me draws him." God alone is responsible for calling us, saving us, and sanctifying us. He is the One who consumes our dying parts and fills us with His character. Striving to forge goodness of character on our own will leave us terribly short of God's design.

For example, we may be successful at avoiding tempting materials or people, but without God we will be unable to contain either the enormous desire or pride growing within us. Or we may strive to harness our anger through our own efforts, but without God we will never completely eradicate all of the pent-up feelings of bitterness, rage, and hurt. We may effectively portray ourselves as godly, selfless, and content, but without God both our families and our private lives may suffer the effects of our lusts.

> *God alone is responsible for calling us, saving us, and sanctifying us.*

God's perfect holiness penetrates every aspect of our lives—whether public or private. Someone once said that the acts we do when no one is watching is what reveals our character. True holiness is demonstrated the same in public as it is in private. Our actions reflect whether our faith is rooted in God, others, or ourselves. Also, our actions establish whether we are motivated by human standards or by intimacy with God.

We have a God who is in control of the sanctification process. The freedom that comes from knowing that is nothing short of spectacular. It sets us free from works and makes us grateful. In a manner of speaking, we can relinquish control and allow Him to proceed with His work in our lives. In doing so, we must be patient and trust that God's character will fill us completely in due time. Trusting in Him means we act on His commands, His direction, and His love. Trusting in God means we willingly lay aside our routines, goals, and desires to rest in Him. As we explore the pruning patterns of God's holiness in our lives, we will briefly examine God's compassion. To experience the full impact of His pruning in our lives, we must understand that He does it with amazing tenderness. When He prunes us, He does so with love.

Touched By His Tenderness

How did we find God? Perhaps some of us recognized our own depravity. Maybe we researched the truth of His Word and came away believing in Him. Even the demons, though, believe in Him. What caused us to accept Him as LORD and Savior? Did we experience emptiness or a desperate need inside that seemed to drive us toward God? Even if we did, what compelled us to allow God to fill us? Why in the world would we be drawn to a Savior who was beaten and placed on a cross—to a God who, even now, is defamed?

When it comes to the practical aspects of Christianity, why would any of us want to follow Christ? Christianity involves suffering, heartache, faith in things not seen, hope in things yet to come, and trust in a God who requires nothing but belief in Him. It sounds like foolishness—and, according to the world, it is. "For the word of the cross is to those who are perishing foolishness, but to us who are being saved it is the power of God" (1 Corinthians 1:18). Since we were all perishing at one time, all of us saw Christ and the message of God as foolishness. To us, as unbelievers, the death and resurrection of Christ was senseless and powerless.

So, the question still remains: why did we turn to God? We did because through God's tenderness and continual prodding, He changed us and called us out of our foolishness to experience His power. Through His loving kindness and nurture, He mysteriously raised us as His children and laid the foundation for our spiritual rebirth.

A poignant display of God's tenderness and His mysterious work in our lives is evidenced in His treatment of the Israelites. In Hosea 11:3-4, we are granted the privilege of seeing things from God's perspective:

> Yet it is I who taught Ephraim (the Northern Kingdom of Israel) to walk; I took them in My arms, but they did not know that I healed them. I led them with cords of a man, with bonds of love, and I became to them as one who lifts the yoke from their jaws; and I bent down and fed them.

In this passage, God expressed perfect love, compassion, and tenderness toward his people. He felt deeply for them. His feelings were much like those of parents toward their young children.

We who were created in His image have compassions and affections that are not human in origin but divine.

Later, in Hosea 11:8b, God conveyed His stirring concern over Israel's rebellion when He said, "My heart is turned over within Me, all My compassions are kindled." God's heart was troubled? His love was burning for them? We do not often think of God feeling like that. However, as an intimately involved parent, God's heart must have ached when Israel turned against Him. Even Jesus expressed tenderness toward Israel when He said, "How often I wanted to gather your children together, just as a hen gathers her brood under her wings" (Luke 13:34b).

Although we have numerous examples of God's tenderness, it is difficult to imagine a powerful, jealous, and omniscient God having sensitive, tender, feelings for us—but He does. We assume these to be human-like feelings, but in reality, we who were created in His image have compassions and affections that are not human in origin but divine.

Those of us who are parents know how compassionately we feel toward our children. God experiences those same feelings, and more, for us. When our babies cry, we feed them. When our little ones are sad and scared at night, we hold them. When they begin to take their first steps, we cheer for them. When they hurt themselves, we tend to them. Chances are that even though our children will never remember these times, they are formative experiences for them. All of the input we have early on is more significant to their development than we may even realize.

According to a recent research study in the *International Herald Tribune,* published by the Center for Research and Human Development at Vanderbilt Medical School, our fundamental reasoning power is established before we have reached our first birthday. In fact, evidence indicates that the single most reliable predictor of our future intellectual ability, accomplishments in school, and success in a vocation is the quantity and to some degree the quality of words a loved one speaks to us before age two. Before children are cognizant of anything, parental impact is profound.

Apparently, the words spoken to children early on in life map their brains for future understanding. They help to determine children's capabilities before cognitive reasoning is functioning. And what are words? What do they represent? Words spoken to children express interest, love, presence, safety, and security. They provide children with meaning, joy, hope, and stability.

Because words communicate those blessings they play a huge role in forming the character, intelligence, and social attachments of growing children.

The study represents a very important spiritual truth as well. It is through the conversations in our formative stages and perhaps through other Christians or the whisperings of the Holy Spirit that we are drawn to God even before discerning who He is. God prepares us before we know or believe in Him. More so than we can ever imagine, we have Him—and only Him—to thank for our salvation and sanctification. Even now He is forming us and changing us through His love, discipline, and continual prodding.

> *Even now He is forming us and changing us through His love, discipline, and continual prodding.*

As we continue exploring the pruning patterns of God's holiness, we must keep in mind that His work in our lives is founded in love. He longs to gather us in His arms to teach us, love us, and cause us to grow and follow Him. As the character of God changes us, marvelous transformations will come into focus. Invariably, people will begin to notice the difference. They will become aware of subtle changes in our character. The winsome and endearing qualities of God will take hold of our lives and penetrate our souls—for God's glory, our own good, and the good of others. It is through the tender act of pruning that God transforms us into His image.

Making Good Friends

The Emperor Moth is one of the most beautiful and largest of all moths. It has a wingspan of about four inches. That is a big moth! The process of hatching from its cocoon proceeds very slowly. First, the moth chews out a narrow opening in the cocoon. Then, it struggles for hours and hours to squeeze its gelatinous body through the hole. If we were to witness an Emperor Moth emerging from its cocoon, we might be tempted to help it and thereby make its struggle less hideous. Our assistance though would cause irreparable damage to the moth. If we enlarged the hole of the cocoon by merely a fraction of a centimeter, the creature would emerge with a large gelatinous body and very tiny wings. God designed the Emperor Moth to struggle through the narrow opening in the cocoon in order to redistribute fluids throughout its body. The struggle itself fills the potential wings with all it needs to be ready to fly after it emerges.

As God's children we are governed by a similar principle. Like the moths, we have certain limits that are necessary to our flight—to our success and abundance. Unless we struggle through them and do what is necessary to stay within those boundaries, we will remain earth-bound, underdeveloped creations of God. In God's perfect plan, we were meant to make spiritual progress within certain boundaries. Our adherence to those limits (His commands) helps to protect us. Boundaries are intended to keep out what could ruin us. Our struggles within those boundaries, which are critical for our spiritual development, produce growth. Throughout Scripture we are provided with boundaries. If we choose to stay within them then we will benefit and grow. If we choose to break the boundaries then we will struggle and suffer setbacks.

One boundary that God addressed involves the relationships we choose to cultivate. Largely, it is our social attachments with people that determine our behavior. Although we would like to believe that our behavior is governed by our values, the primary determinant of our behavior is not our values but our closeness. More often than not, we will willingly sacrifice our values on the altar of human closeness. Being created as relational beings that crave love, power, and fulfillment, oftentimes we adapt our values to fit our environment or our social groups. Concisely stated:

- Most of us believe that: our **values** determine, our behavior
- When in truth: our **closeness** determines, our behavior

Most of us believe that our values determine our behavior, when in truth, our closeness determines our behavior

---

In time, our social interactions and closeness—whether positive or negative—will begin to reflect who we are and how we act. The Bible says, "Do not be bound together with unbelievers" (II Corinthians 6:14a). Scripture admonishes us to select friends and mates who have similar values, and this has nothing to do with exclusivity or favoritism. Developing relationships with people of different backgrounds, races, nationalities, and even different religions can be an immensely rewarding experience. If we only associate with people who share our opinions, experiences, perceptions, or prejudices, then the work of God in our lives is severely limited along with our impact on others. However, surrounding ourselves with people who continually compromise or disrespect our values can be devastating to our spiritual growth and intimacy with God. Likewise, it can markedly influence our actions.

For example, approximately five million children in the world are starving to death right now. Yet, we in the United States spend three billion dollars on pet food annually. That three billion dollars could go a long way toward solving the human hunger problem, but our action is based on closeness rather than values. Most of us wholeheartedly believe that it is more important to feed a starving child than to feed a pet. We interact with our pets and in doing so draw close to them. On the other hand, few of us are normally in the company of starving children. If we allow God to draw us close to those kids then our behavior will change.

Carl Sandburg, an American writer and poet in the early 1900s said, "I have an eagle in me that wants to soar, and I have a hippo in me that wants to wallow in the mud." Both tendencies are in our hearts as well. The determining factors will be the direction in which we decide to go and the relationships we choose to build.

As parents, one of our important responsibilities is to monitor the friendships of our children. We taught our sons to seek relationships with people who challenge and encourage their spiritual, psychological, social, and intellectual growth. Just as children must be taught how to read, write, pray, practice good manners, make wise decisions, and drive a car, they must also be taught how to choose friends and relate to people.

If they begin hanging around those who are ushering them away from Jesus Christ, we have the responsibility to intervene. I know that it may feel awkward because it seems invasive, but actually it is a loving response. As parents we are to provide accountability, direction, and discipline for them, just as Jesus does with us. When our children are involved in compromising relationships, we can say to them, "The people you've been spending time with do not seem to be encouraging you toward Christ. They are bringing you down. What are your thoughts about that?" By letting our children consider this behavior, we allow God the opportunity to work directly with our children before we have to act. If we only receive an emotional response or sense little spiritual awareness in our children, then we need to say, "I can't tell you who you can or can't make friends with, but I can limit the time you spend with them. I understand that at your age you are more likely to make friends on an emotional level rather than on a spiritual basis. Since I love you, I am going to help." We can and should set boundaries to limit the interaction our children have with those who are making them weaker people.

Each of my sons has asked me on more than one occasion; "Don't you trust me?" I would usually respond rather quickly, "Of course I don't trust you. Are you kidding me? I'm 50 and I don't trust me! Why would I trust a 16-year-old?" The point is, we are all human and sinful. Adults are no different—but hopefully wiser.

Because we care, we must seek to cultivate healthy friendships of our own and we must also provide our children with instruction. While they are in our home, we have a responsibility to guard them from harmful relationships and to encourage them to pursue challenging, deep friendships.

Focusing on the best in all of life helps them develop confidence. So, I do not emphasize concerns about all the "bad stuff" that can happen. Instead, both my wife and I emphasize excellence with the hope that their lives will be wonderful instruments for Christ to use in this world.

My Favorite Things

In addition to carefully watching the types of friendships that our children and we pursue, we must also determine what materials to exclude. Like the people who draw us away from God, some materials can also cause great harm. In fact, the type of materials we take into our lives can have a much greater consequence than we imagined.

Different types of materials tempt each of us. One of the ways to determine our weak spots is to recognize what naturally draws our attention. For instance, some of us find that the pursuit of knowledge pulls us away from God and His purpose. Because we are filling our minds with all sorts of knowledge, intimacy with God is sacrificed for information. Others of us involve ourselves in harmful conversations or gossip. Some of us occupy our leisure time by watching movies or reading materials that are not uplifting. Because of our varied personalities and environmental influences, our propensities toward certain types of material gratification are individually unique.

For example, I am predisposed to alcoholism because it is in my family. I am, however, not tempted to drink liquor since that would be a big danger for me. I know the danger is real because twice in college after drinking just a single beer, I was dancing around the room with a lampshade on my head. That image alone makes the idea of taking a drink extremely unappealing.

Oddly enough, a much more real temptation for me than alcohol is the temptation to spend too much time playing solitaire on my computer. I actually had to delete the game from my database.

That which distracts each of us from our doing or being our best for God needs to be eliminated from our lives. Satan is the most subtle and devious of all God's creation. To combat him and the sin within us, we must watch our lives for the subtleties of sin and at the same time guard ourselves from the more obvious temptations. When we do discover our trouble spots, we must run from them. Romans 6:13a reads, "And do not go on presenting the members of your body to sin as instruments of unrighteousness." While we may have the option to return to sin, as Christians we also have the power to shut down that particular temptation in our lives. Some of us may need to take radical steps to break free from material temptations, and to instill some severe safeguards in our lives to protect ourselves.

In Homer's *The Odyssey*, Odysseus traveled beyond the island of the Sirens. The Sirens were sea nymphs who sang enchanting songs to passing mariners. Many seafarers who heard the songs were lured toward them and crashed onto the island rocks. To avoid the possibility of heeding their call and grounding his boat on the rocks, Odysseus had his crew strap him to the mast of the ship. As a result, he could not respond to the Sirens' calls. He also had the crew put wax in their own ears so that they could not hear their songs. His actions demonstrated remarkable self-control and foresight.

We, too, must be willing to take steps to avoid temptation. For example, if we struggle with lustful temptations that arise from our Internet use, we could institute a security system on our computers to prevent access to such sites. If we struggle with watching certain programs on television, we could involve other people in our lives to keep us accountable or we could even remove the television altogether.

Whatever our temptations, it is crucial that we take action to reduce their stronghold in our lives. Often, it requires drastic action. Jesus said, "He who loves his life loses it; and he who hates his life in this world shall keep it to life eternal" (John 12:25). We must actively turn away from all that will bring us down.

So, what is it going to take to accomplish the will of God in our lives? What are some ways we can get close to God? Both of these goals can be approached by reading the Bible, praying, communing with others, worshiping, learning about God through books, tapes, or radio, enjoying His creation, creating art, or talking with a spiritual mentor.

In our battle with temptations, we should be aware that God is the One who gives us the power to overcome. It may take time to remove the temptations from our lives, but God's strength and timing make it an ultimately attainable goal. Our task is to yield to Him, persevere, and trust in His work even in the thick of our struggle.

> No temptation has seized you except what is common to man. And God is faithful; He will not let you be tempted beyond what you can bear. But when you are tempted, He will also provide a way out so that you can stand up under it. (I Corinthians 10:13 NIV)

Don't Make Me Angry!

The Incredible Hulk had an inflated ego. Do you remember the old television show staring Bill Bixby and Lou Ferrigno? Whenever Bill Bixby (the runaway scientist) was provoked to anger he would transform into the Incredible Hulk, a hideous beast played by Lou Ferrigno. It was interesting that it really did not take much to make the scientist angry. For instance, at the beginning of nearly every episode he unwittingly wandered into some shady establishment merely needing to use the telephone or grab a bite to eat. Invariably, several hoodlums looking to stir up trouble would accost him. In the midst of his harassment, Bixby would utter his infamous words, "Don't make me angry. You wouldn't like me when I'm angry."

The problem was, he was quick to anger. If they looked at him the wrong way, he got angry. If they insulted him, he got angry. If they pushed him, he got angry. Invariably he would end up being thrown through a wall, behind a counter, or out a door, and then the scientist was transformed and emerged as the angry, great, green, Incredible Hulk. By the end of the brawl, the establishment was practically destroyed and the hoodlums lay bruised and perplexed on the floor.

In a manner of speaking, many of us are inclined to believe in the Incredible Hulk myth before we believe in God's power. That is, we will use our anger to gain control over a situation before submitting to God's control. We believe anger to be our trump card. When people or circumstances around us begin to get out of our control, we may think or say aloud, "Okay, I'm going to get angry pretty soon. Things had better straighten up fast!" In fact, we often use anger to reduce the uncertainty in our lives and alleviate our emotional pain. But "the anger of man does not achieve the righteousness of God" (James 1:20).

While God may express His anger as well, it is not His primary way of moving in our lives and in the world. His power is seldom displayed in torrents of angry justice; rather, it is displayed in showers of mercy. Hidden beneath our calm Christian persona is the faulty belief that getting mad enough about bad things will improve the world (or at least help our circumstances). However, it does not. Our anger only breeds more anger. Still, we use it to get what we want and may even enjoy using it.

How often are we angry? How important is anger in our lives? We might be surprised by our answers. If we are quick to subdue our anger or laugh it off, we may not notice its prevalence in our lives.

In The Orlando Sentinel newspaper, there is a designated "Ticked-Off" section. People write in and describe various conflicts that made them angry throughout the week. Then, the newspaper publishes their responses. It started out as a single section, once a week. Now, there are additional "Ticked-Off" sections in the sports pages and in the teenagers' section. People get enjoyment out of reading what makes others mad. They can identify with it. We can all probably identify with it.

However, anger is a serious issue to God. Anger destroys relationships. Jesus said:

> You have heard that the ancients were told "You shall not commit murder and whoever commits murder shall be liable to the court." But I say to you that everyone who is angry with his brother shall be guilty before the court…. If therefore you are presenting your offering at the altar, and there remember that your brother has something against you, leave your offering there before the altar, and go your way; first be reconciled to your brother, and then come and present your offering. (Matthew 5:21-24)

We cannot fool God. Behavior can hide or reveal who we really are, but God looks at the heart. He knows us. The words that Jesus spoke communicate the serious consequences of our anger. Not only does it drive a wedge between the injured person and us, but it also affects our relationship with God. God is the Alpha and Omega of our reconciliation with our brothers. When we fail to forgive another person or apologize for our actions, we sever our link with God and close off a part of ourselves from Him because God is not detached from our relationships with others. The hope we have for reconciliation with our brothers is God. And the hope we have for restoration of our relationship with God is reconciliation with our brothers.

God is very much aware that we all will experience occasional bursts of anger. It can be a natural reaction to disturbances in our lives. Even Jesus justly expressed His anger when He was with us in human form (John 2:12-16). However, in Matthew 5, Jesus spoke about a type of anger that is nurtured.

This anger smolders and is fed by our bitterness, lack of forgiveness, and pride. It is an anger that is like a virus running rampant throughout our bodies. Over time it takes over our lives. By refusing to forgive another or confess our hurtful actions, we end up making prisoners of ourselves. In fact, some of us lay in bed at night feeling the effects of unresolved anger. We brood over situations where people have hurt us. Even years after a conflict, our anger toward another can resurface as if it was yesterday, but Jesus wants us to get rid of that anger. He instructed us to, "Be angry, and yet do not sin" (Ephesians 4:26a). Seeking to understand why we are angry and bringing our anger to God can release us and begin the healing process.

Often, it is when we recognize that we have the same propensities to cause harm to others that we can begin to forgive and let go. Through seeking a godly perspective of our situation, God can help us understand enough to relinquish our control and let Him lead. Whenever we experience an impasse with anger we should ask ourselves, "How would God want me to respond?" Since He has given us His character, what is getting in the way of responding like He would?

Some Quarrel

In addition to our battle with anger, we also have a tendency to dispute with one another and be quarrelsome. Often then, quarrels lead to anger. Our position as God's children is to avoid quarrels. In 2 Timothy 2:14, the Apostle Paul gave this instruction to Timothy, a young church leader:

> Remind them (the believers in the church) of these things, and solemnly charge them in the presence of God not to wrangle about words, which is useless, and leads to the ruin of the hearers.

Today, words can be twisted and redefined to mean almost anything. For some of us it is easy to get caught up in the debate over words, ideas, and theories. Paul instructed us to avoid such discussions no matter how important they may seem to us, because God is in control. He said:

> But refuse foolish and ignorant speculations, knowing that they produce quarrels. And the LORD's bondservant must not be quarrelsome, but be kind to all, able to teach, patient when wronged, with gentleness correcting those who are in opposition. (2 Timothy 2:23-25a)

The word "refuse" in this passage literally means "just say no." In other words, it is totally within our power to do something about these situations. In this passage, Paul was specifically referring to an argument that arose in the church about some minor details of Jewish heritage. This truth, however, stands for all details within all topics. We are to avoid being mixed up in quarrels over words, details, and foggy speculations. Instead, by pursuing kindness and gentleness rather than our own agenda, we will discover God's power at work within us and our hearers. We can safely avoid the entrapping quagmire of details and speculations that lead to anger and further sin.

An old *Uncle Remus* story about Brer Rabbit and the Tar Baby illustrates the danger of quarrels rather well. In the story, Brer Rabbit was hopping along the road when he came across a large lump of tar sitting on a log. He was unaware that Brer Fox and Brer Bear had dressed it up to look like a person. As Brer Rabbit hopped by the Tar Baby, he said, "Howdy!" But the Tar Baby said nothing. Brer Rabbit stopped in his tracks and glared at the Tar Baby, waiting for it to respond. He then said, "What's the matter with you? I said, 'Howdy.' Is you deaf? If you is, I can holler louder." Still, the Tar Baby didn't respond. Finally, Brer Rabbit got so mad that he socked the lump of tar in the nose. When his hand stuck in the tar, he became furious and hit it again with his other fist. By the time he was finished, Brer Rabbit was so stuck in tar that he could "scarcely move his eyeballs."

Like Brer Rabbit, we too can get stuck. The more we try to iron out the details of speculations or debate over half-truths, the more stuck we will get. Vain disputes about words and debates over who is right or wrong usually degenerate into messy quarrels.

In his letter to Timothy, Paul not only instructed him to avoid quarrels but he also tried to prepare Timothy for the inevitable development of them. Like a wise grandfather, Paul explained that regardless of our good actions there always will be some kind of wrong reaction or misunderstanding. Paul's strategy for Timothy was to plan for disputes ahead of time by deciding how to respond and by avoiding the natural passions that spring from within. We, too, have to plan ahead of time not to argue the details. Our job is not only to avoid foolish arguments, but we are also to be patient and maintain a long-term, godly view. The pressure that we place on ourselves is lifted when we understand that God's plans will be executed regardless of our success or failure in an argument. In truth, if we really understood and sincerely believed in Him, we would spend a lot less time arguing and a lot more time praying.

One of the primary reasons we are caught in quarrels, angry disputes, and their repercussions is because we take ourselves too seriously. Failing to trust in God and His holiness, we have lifted our conflicts, problems, and mistakes to a loftier height than is necessary or accurate. However, our actions and mistakes will never change God's love for us or His work in our lives and the lives of others.

I receive a half dozen calls a week from people who believe that their actions have caused irreparable harm to themselves or others. They believe that they have destroyed their lives. Sometimes they are totally overwrought and begin the conversation with, "I have ruined my life and I'm thinking about ending it all."

My first response is usually not, "Oh please, think this through. Tell me what happened." Instead, I try to respond to them with a grandfather's perspective. I say, "No you didn't. You didn't ruin your life. Whatever it is, life is bigger than that." It is true! Life is a big, long, deal!

We all make mistakes that affect others and hurt us. In fact, some errors may be very significant, bold sins, but they will not ruin our lives unless we allow them to do so. In order to make it through the tough times, the quarrels, and disputes, we must adopt a grandfather's perspective. It is a long-term perspective. It says, "God forgives and He is bigger than my mistakes, my actions, and my problems. This, too, shall pass!" As we begin to respond to anger in a godly fashion, avoid quarrels and disputes, and view life from a grandfather's perspective, we may be able to avoid a bitter and vengeful spirit that results from anger in our lives.

The Sour Taste of Sweet Revenge!

Something of vengeance I had tasted for the first time;
as aromatic wine it seemed, on swallowing, warm and racy:
its after-flavour, metallic and corroding,
gave me a sensation as if I had been poisoned.
— Charlotte Brontë (1816–55), English novelist

In Shakespeare's *Merchant of Venice*, there is a character named Shylock who was a Jewish moneychanger. Throughout his life, Shylock had experienced horrible discrimination in his community. The years of pain had taken a toll on him, creating a bitter, angry, and frustrated man. At one point in the story, a Christian man named Antonio became indebted to him by a contract. Finally, Shylock had the opportunity to vent his years of accumulated bitterness on this one man, Antonio. In the court ruling, the judge agreed that based on their contract, Shylock was legally permitted to exact a "pound of flesh" from Antonio. However, since the contract did not include blood, the judge ruled that Shylock could have his pound of flesh if he could cut it away without spilling any blood. If he could not do that, he would lose everything.

In our anger and bitterness we often seek revenge on other people, either deliberately or unknowingly. Like Shylock, by responding only to our fleshly inclination we fail to see the importance of the blood and ultimately end up defeated. When we disregard the far-reaching effects of revenge on our lives and on the lives of others, we blindly perpetuate the problem. In addition, the intensity of our angry and vengeful spirit prevents us from fully considering the reason for the other people's actions. There is always more to our conflicts with others than that which is readily apparent.

The Bible says, "For our struggle is not against flesh and blood, but against the rulers, against the powers, against the world forces of this darkness, against the spiritual forces of wickedness in the heavenly places" (Ephesians 6:12). When people hurt us, more than likely they do not have a personal vendetta against us. Instead, their actions are deeply rooted in their own life experiences, hurt, and pain. Our retaliation will not help resolve these issues for them or us.

Most of us are familiar with the following verses:

> And if a man injures his neighbor, just as he has done, so it shall be done to him: fracture for fracture, eye for eye, tooth for tooth; just as he has injured a man, so it shall be inflicted on him. (Leviticus 24:19-20)

Even while most of us do not apply the words literally (I hope), we do tend to understand them as personal instructions. That is, we interpret them to mean that God sanctions personal retaliation. He does not.

The Bible never condones or justifies our revenge. In fact, the "eye for an eye" passage indicates a significant upgrade in the fairness that retribution had been missing. It replaced an unwritten code that was understood to be more like "death for an eye" than "eye for an eye." Beyond that, however, the law in Leviticus was designed to be a community judgment, not a personal judgment. Individuals who were harmed were never permitted to exact a personal judgment on the perpetrators. The law demanded the judgment to be a community decision and admonished fair treatment of the accused.

Jesus Christ fulfilled the law and further explained it to His disciples and followers when He said:

> You have heard that it was said, "An eye for an eye, and a tooth for a tooth." But I say to you, do not resist him who is evil; but whoever

slaps you on your right cheek, turn to him the other also. (Matthew 5:38-39)

His words do not imply that we should let people injure us physically in a fight. In fact, further examination reveals that He was not talking about a physical fight, but about insults. Jesus was instructing us not to retaliate when we are insulted, but to respond in love. Our response to insults and attacks should be proactive—not simply reactive. That is because we understand that He is the Judge and we trust that He knows what is best. He has a wonderful plan for our lives and even as we experience suffering He increases our strength and maturity.

There is an old phrase, "What doesn't kill you will make you stronger." I believe that is true. Being a Christian means that we suffer for Christ through insults, pain, and heartache. We can choose to succumb to that pain, allowing it to infect us with its bitter and angry venom, or we can trust in the "antidote" of Scripture, believing that a loving and God-focused response sets us free. While He grieves with us in our pain, God is also at work even in the lives of those who hurt us. Though there are always consequences for actions, God, through His love, desires to transform not only our lives, but also the lives of those who hurt us.

As our relationship with God deepens, we come to grips with our own depravity and realize that those who hurt us are not the only people who have a propensity to cause harm. We recognize that we have been just as rebellious and callous as the people who have caused us harm. Not seeking revenge demonstrates and strengthens our faith in God. If we respond in love we can actively partake in the steady transformation of other people's lives. In humility, we will be able to see that the consequences of blessing someone who has done us harm far outweigh the repercussions of any vengeful actions.

In an excellent book called *Front Porch Tales,* Philip Gulley, a Quaker preacher in Indianapolis writes about his childhood. He introduces us to people he knew while growing up in a small town. One story involves the town doctor: When Doc was not tending folks, he was usually out enjoying his favorite hobby—planting trees. He loved to plant trees, but had a strange method. In the odd philosophy of horticulture husbandry, Doc must have been schooled in the "no pain, no gain" approach. Whenever he planted a tree, he did not water it. In fact, he went beyond that. Each morning, he would roll up an old newspaper, walk over to the newly planted tree, and begin beating the trunk. One day, the author saw his weird behavior and asked him about it. Doc said, "I'm just gettin' the tree's attention right here."

Philip then said, "I've noticed that you don't water your trees. Why not?"

The Doc looked up at him and said, "Cause it would spoil them!" Philip was still perplexed, so Doc explained, "You know, when all the water is at the surface, the roots don't go deep. And if the roots don't go deep, you don't have a strong tree."

Later, Philip attempted to plant some trees on his own. Not adhering to the Doc's strange philosophy, he watered them every day. They became flimsy, weak and pliable trees. Whenever he walked past Doc's property, he could not help but admire his fine, tall trees. It occurred to him that they were strong because they had deep roots. Applying that knowledge to his spiritual life, he wrote this: "I used to kneel by my boys' bedsides while they were sleeping and pray that God would spare them from the hurt of the world. Now, I don't pray that any more. I pray that they will have deep roots."

Deep roots in our relationship with God only develop from persevering through the pains of trials and testing. When we resist God's work in our hearts, we are like grains of seed scattered among rocky places—growing for a short time, then withering for lack of root. We may initially grow quickly and seem mature, but without the roots of God's truth and strength, the troubles and persecutions of the world will easily tear us down. However, following Christ's example, seeking God for support, and persevering through the trials will produce deep roots. As we mature, we just may be granted the joy of witnessing how our loving actions have positively affected those around us.

Before the Berlin Wall was torn down, there was an incident at the wall initiated by the East Berliners. In the Communist block a group of people gathered all of the rank garbage they could find and put it on a truck. In the middle of the night, they backed the truck to the wall and dumped the garbage onto the Western side. In the morning, many West Berliners awoke to a hideous smell. Upon seeing the garbage, they cleaned it up and then planned their response. Three days later, at the very site on the eastern side of the wall, they deposited loaves of freshly baked bread, utensils, clean garments, and other goods that were necessary for a wonderful daily life. With it, they placed a note that said, "You can only give what you have." Ironically, not long after that, the wall between the two sides was removed—literally.

As followers of Christ, we have more than enough to give. We have been given more than enough to simply cope. We do not have to respond, "an eye for an eye" or "a tooth for a tooth." We can respond as Jesus Christ has to us—with mercy and love. As Christians, we have something far better to give to others than anything they could ever give us: we have the love of Christ.

We Must Lust Less

What resides in our hearts is every bit as important as what comes out of our mouths or what we do with our bodies. In the greatest sermon ever preached, the Sermon on the Mount, Jesus pointed out that it is not just our actions that count, but our motivation behind those actions. In Matthew 5:27-28, Jesus said:

> You have heard that it was said, 'You shall not commit adultery;' but I say to you, that everyone who looks on a woman to lust for her has committed adultery with her already in his heart.

Often, I have heard people say, "Wow! Since the Bible says it is wrong to even think bad thoughts, I might as well go ahead and take action anyway." What a terrible mistake to make that choice! Certainly God holds us accountable when we entertain evil thoughts, but when we actually perform them, the effect on other people's lives—as well as on our own life—is devastating. I have seen marriages and families torn apart by one person's decision to act on private evil thoughts. The sobering truth is, our evil thoughts will not remain in the thought realm forever. Continuing to entertain them will eventually lead us to action. Jesus knew that and we must realize it as well.

I have already mentioned that Jesus recognized that we would occasionally experience brief flashes of anger. The same holds true for sexual attraction. Depending on the circumstance and the condition of our hearts at the time, we may or may not need to ask for forgiveness. For instance, the last thing a pubescent boy or girl needs to feel is condemnation for experiencing a physical attraction toward someone or for wrestling with sexual feelings. To some extent, that is a natural part of growing up.

Likewise, a mature adult who recognizes the physical attractiveness of another person is not sinning. In fact, the attraction can be quite natural. Throughout our lives, we will probably be physically attracted to certain types of people. We do not plan it. Our hormones are indiscriminate, and they will always be indiscriminate. That is a part of life. Therefore, we should not be shocked or overreact when that attraction happens.

> *God holds us accountable when we entertain evil thoughts, but when we actually perform them, the effect on other people's lives—as well as on our own life—is devastating.*

What Jesus was referring to is that when we nurse thoughts and respond to the sin in our hearts we are voluntarily entertaining lust. The original Greek words that are translated, "looks on a woman to lust" denote purpose. He was not referring to merely a quick glance or a passing thought. He was concerned about our tendency to pursue lust in our thoughts. Why? Because as a man "thinks within himself, so he is" (Proverbs 23:7). And the fuel for our thoughts comes from our hearts. The sad and often disregarded truth is that nursing lustful thoughts leads to action because this re-energizes the fallen state of our hearts and beckons our sin natures to resurface.

In order to combat the powerful force of the sin in our
hearts, Jesus provided us with a radical and painful intervention:

> And if your right eye makes you stumble, tear it out and throw it
> from you; for it is better for you that one of the parts of your body
> perish, than for your whole body to be thrown into hell. (Matthew
> 5:29)

He reiterated the same instructions with regard to our hands
as well. These are very radical and graphic instructions.

We should keep in mind that Jesus was using a metaphor
and a type of shock therapy to stress His point. He wanted us
to fully understand the severity of the sin and our desperate
need for radical action. When we find ourselves struggling
with lust, the solution needs to be extreme and painful
because it is not about our behavior but about the condition
of our hearts. In order to keep our hearts open and yielded to
God, we must be aware of our thoughts and motivations and
we must continually allow God to expose and consume those
decaying parts. It is a lifelong venture and our hearts will never
be completely pure until God brings us home.

Jeremiah 17:9 says, "The heart is more deceitful than all
else and is desperately sick; who can understand it?" We must
become aware of the recurring pattern of our hearts—to
create things to desire. Just as in the old days when people
created idols, so we use our minds and hearts to create sex
symbols and objects of lust. This stark understanding of our
own depravity brings us face-to-face with the fact that we are
the makers of things to desire. And, we have created some
pretty silly and often distasteful stuff! I was reminded of this
just recently.

One Thursday evening, Becky and I spent six hours in the
middle of the Altamonte Mall. Typically, I go to the mall only
to browse through the bookstore for a few minutes. I walk

into the bookstore, find some books, buy them, and then head out. So, why were we at the mall for six hours? Well, my youngest son, Joel, had a part-time job working at a snow cone vending booth at the center of the mall. On that particular night, he had a very important commitment that conflicted with his work schedule. So, being a super-diligent kid, he found a substitute to work for him. Ten minutes before Joel's shift was to begin, the sub called Joel and backed out of it.

Becky and I had just returned from work. After Joel told us what happened, Becky and I looked at each other—the only communication we needed. I said, "Doing the icy stuff in the mall could be fun. We'll fill in for you." Joel was ecstatic!

The three of us jumped into the car and rushed to the mall. Joel took advantage of the short ride and explained our job duties. When we got there, he spent a few minutes showing us how to operate everything and then took off.

The whole experience turned out to be kind of fun. Really, it was. It was entertaining to watch the people—some passing by and others stopping at our booth. Most of those who stopped, spent a long time choosing from the 100 flavoring options we offered for their snow cones. As the evening progressed, several people from the church came by and after doing double takes bought snow cones and chatted. The whole experience was great!

During our six-hour shift, while becoming proficient at snow cone artistry, Becky and I became aware of some interesting clothing fads. One fad really puzzled me and I am still not sure what to think of it. It has to do with clothing made to show off your belly button. What is that all about, anyway? Please understand that I am not mad about this. I got a belly button. You got a belly button. All God's children got belly buttons. Adam and Eve did not have a belly button, but all of the rest of us do. Anyway, I just could not figure out for the life of me why all of these belly buttons were visible. I understand that God made our bodies attractive, but they are also fallen—some of those belly buttons were more fallen than others. I assume the whole belly button thing is supposed to be sexy. What is next—turning our eyelids inside out?

Many of our created temptations are ridiculous, but in our sin nature, we are attracted to that which is very shallow. We have become wrapped up in our lusts—lusts that indicate the condition of our hearts. Invariably, pursuing our own lusts will come to a very bad end.

If we struggle with particular sins, we need to realize that those weak parts will never be completely fixed until we are in heaven. Still, by refusing to nurse lustful thoughts, we can successfully avoid falling into temptation. We need to some-how determine the steps we must take to get our thought lives under control. Those who struggle with pornography found in magazines, videos, and even romance novels can begin to move away from lust by destroying the pornographic material.

Sadly, scandalous relationships outside of marriage are not uncommon. When these happen, love for God as well as spouses is compromised. And when affairs occur with people at our workplaces, reassignment or even firing may result. Other "solutions" may include choosing to resign our jobs and, if necessary, a move to another city or state. That is radical! It is also painful. However, as God's children, radical steps must be taken when the situation becomes threatening to our spiritual maturity, family, and our relationship with God. Jesus Christ's death on the cross was radical because He knew the effect that sin has on our lives. His importance to us will determine our radical steps toward victory. Satan takes drastic measures to capture our minds and hearts—so we must take radical measures to avoid him.

Surrendering to God

The exciting truth about Jesus is that He willingly walked into the baited trap for us, paid the penalty, and showed us the way to freedom. Whether it is our anger, bitterness, quarrelsome spirit, vengeful attitude, or consuming lust that we must relinquish, we know that He asks us to do it because He has something much better for us. Thankfully, we have a Father in heaven who will not ask us to sacrifice anything that He is not ready to replace countless times over. Unlike the bait of Satan, God's gift is real and eternal. It completely fulfills us. By relinquishing our worldly treasures and idols we can experience the gift that never dies. The following story makes the point well:

A little girl walked with her mother as they passed an old five-and-dime store. The owners had recently received a shipment of pop-beads and were displaying them in the window. Even though they were only plastic and a sure-to-be-short-lived fad, the girl was absolutely crazy about pop-beads.

She tugged on her mother's sleeve. "Oh mommy! I've just got to have those pop-beads. Would you buy them for me?"

The mother looked at her and smiled. "Honey, I don't think I should get them for you just because you saw them and decided you must have them right now." The girl's expression began to melt. The mother knelt down beside her. "Still, you are getting old enough to start earning an allowance. I'm sure your father and I can think of some ways to put you to work around the house so you can earn some money." The little girl beamed.

That night, she told her father what happened and how she wanted to earn money around the house. So, he put her to work. It was not too long before she earned enough money for a pop-bead necklace since they cost only about 69 cents. As soon as she received her allowance, she hurried to the five-and-dime store, bought the necklace, and immediately placed it around her neck. She could not wait to go to school and show it to all of her friends.

The next day, all of the kids admired her new necklace and told her how beautiful she looked. Some even said it made her look older. By the time she arrived home she felt like she was on top of the world. That night when her father walked in the door, he looked at his daughter and said, "There's my princess. You look gorgeous. And look at that jewelry, oh my!" The little girl blushed and hugged her daddy tightly.

After supper, she took a bath—all the while wearing her necklace. Then she put on her pajamas and climbed into her father's lap as he sat in his big chair by the fireplace. This night, as was the routine every night, they spent a few moments talking with each other and then after praying, he kissed her on the cheek and sent her to bed.

One night, a few weeks after her necklace purchase, after they prayed, her father kissed her, paused for a moment and asked, "Honey, do you love me?"

The little girl smiled at him, "Of course I love you, daddy."

He responded, "Then give me your pop-beads."

The girl was shocked. She forced a smile and chuckled, "Boys don't wear pop-beads!" Her father did not smile. Quickly, she hopped down and went to bed.

The next day, still wearing her necklace, she went to school. Everybody continued to compliment her. That night, when her dad came home, she was a little bit quieter. After following through the routine—eating supper, taking her bath, and putting on her pajamas, she went to her father and slowly climbed on his lap. They talked for a few moments. Then he prayed and kissed her. Right before the little girl hopped down, he asked her the same question he had asked the previous night. "Honey, do you love me?"

"Daddy, I really do love you." Her eyes cautiously searched his.

He replied, "Then give me your pop-beads."

Her face grew serious. "I can't! I can't!" She jumped from his lap and ran to her bedroom.

Another school day followed. She felt somewhat sad even though a few kids were still commenting on her pretty necklace. After coming home, eating supper, and completing the nightly routine, she went straight to bed. She did not sit with her father though he waited for her. She could not stand to hear the question again. She could not bear to face a decision like that. The next night, she did the same thing. She went through the routine, but did not sit with her father. After several days of avoiding him she finally could endure the pain no longer. Not talking with her father was more than she could bear. So, when she came home that day, she ate supper, went through the routine, and hopped in her father's lap. After he prayed and kissed her he asked the same dreaded question. "Honey, do you love me?"

The girl replied, "Yes daddy, I do!"

"Then give me your pop-beads." He held out his hand.

This time, the little girl took them from around her neck and gave them to him. Her father threw them into the fire. The little girl sobbed as she watched them melt. He gently stroked her hair and held her while she cried, then reaching into his coat pocket, he pulled out a beautiful string of real pearls. He fastened them around her neck, and said, "I love you, too."

We have a Father who loves us dearly. We know where to find Him. He has something far better for us than what we think is important. We may believe that we cannot live without our creature comforts or our emotional crutches, but God has a gift for us that is unsurpassable in brilliance and beauty. The only question is, are we willing to take the chance on Him?

Prayer of Holiness

"Holiness does not consist in mystic speculations, enthusiastic fervours, or uncommanded austerities; it consists in thinking as God thinks, and willing as God wills."

—*John Brown*
19th century Scottish theologian

CHAPTER FIVE

There are thoughts which are prayers.
There are moments when, whatever the posture of the body,
the soul is on its knees.

—Victor Hugo

*P*rayer is simple and it is the communication pathway to God. Often, though, when we think about praying our minds and flesh resist—as if prayer is an arduous task. These kinds of thought may cross our minds:

- I just do not know what to say to God.

- God knows my heart already, so telling Him anything seems useless.

- My prayers will not be effective, because I do not have enough faith yet.

- There is not enough time to pray right now.

Our faulty expectations and/or perceptions tend to make us helpless and hopeless in our prayer lives, yet that is exactly where God wants us. King David wrote in Psalm 131:1-2:

> O LORD, my heart is not proud, nor my eyes haughty; nor do I involve myself in great matters, or in things too difficult for me. Surely I have composed and quieted my soul; like a weaned child rests against his mother, my soul is like a weaned child within me.

Our helplessness is an essential element of prayer because we all experience pain. King David was no exception and rather than hide from it, he acknowledged his pain and admitted his folly to the LORD. In Psalm 51, David said that God does not delight in our sacrifices but in our moldable and repentant hearts. As Jesus instructed us to pray in Matthew 6, He continued with the familiar theme—prayer is simple and sure. He taught us how to speak simply to our great Father.

Simple Words and Simple Saints

> And when you are praying, do not use meaningless repetition, as the Gentiles do, for they suppose that they will be heard for their many words. Therefore do not be like them; for your Father knows what you need, before you ask Him (Matthew 6:7-8).

Jesus knew that it does not take very long for the right activities and even the right motivations to get lost in human self-centeredness. He knew that as we talk with God, it is only a matter of time before we start to fall in love with our own voices. So, Jesus' instruction to us was to keep it short! The longer the prayer, the tougher it is to concentrate on the original purpose: to have a conversation with God instead of a monologue to Him.

Throughout history, it has been the human tendency in every religion to have lengthy prayers. For some reason, we view long prayers as sacrificial, powerful, and persuasive. God does not—He values the state of our hearts. We do not need to convince God of anything. He already knows what we need and we cannot change His perfect will for us. He not only has the correct answer; He has the best answer.

> *We do not need to convince God of anything. He already knows what we need and we cannot change His perfect will for us.*

In 1 Kings 18, there is a wonderful example of a "pagan" prayer. During that time in Bible history, Israel had abandoned the LORD's command and was worshiping a pagan god. On Mount Carmel, Elijah challenged 450 prophets of the god, Baal, to demonstrate their god's power. He told them to prepare a sacrifice and pray to their god. Likewise, he would pray to his God. Whichever god answered with fire would be deemed the true God. So the prophets of Baal began praying. They called to their god from morning until noon. They danced wildly upon the altar, as was the custom. But no voice responded and the sacrifice was not consumed.

Then Elijah said to them, "Call out with a loud voice, for he is a god; either he is occupied or gone aside, or is on a journey, or perhaps he is asleep and needs to be awakened" (I Kings 18:27). With that, the prophets cried louder and cut themselves until they bled, according to their custom. They tried many things to get Baal's attention. The mid-day passed while they raved frantically until the time of the evening sacrifice. From morning until night they mounted up their words, yet nothing happened.

Finally, in stepped Elijah and all of the people drew close as he assembled twelve stones, placed wood upon them, and prepared the sacrifice. Next, he dug a trench around the altar and then ordered the people to fill four large jars with water and to pour it on the wood as well as the offering. This they did three times, according to Elijah's command, and when they finished the altar was soaked and water filled the trench. Then Elijah said,

> O LORD, the God of Abraham, Isaac and Israel, today let it be known that Thou art God in Israel, and that I am Thy servant, and that I have done all these things at Thy word. Answer me, O LORD, answer me, that this people may know that Thou, O LORD, art God, and that Thou hast turned their hearts back again. (I Kings 18:36-37)

At that moment, fire sent by God fell from the sky and consumed the burnt offering, the wood, the stones, the dust, and all of the water in and around the altar.

For the prophets of Baal, all of their words, sacrifices, and customs amounted to nothing. Their prayers failed because they depended upon their own politics of god—their own activities and their own words. In essence, they worshiped the wrong god. But the most effective prayer, a simple one prayed by Elijah, called down the power of God. Elijah did not need to coax God or impress Him. He simply needed to pray.

There is an old principle in scientific theory called *Ockham's Razor*. It asserts that when we are faced with more than one alternative, the correct answer is usually the simplest explanation. The principle not only applies to science but to prayer as well. When we use unnecessary verbiage in our prayers, we end up complicating our requests. Neither our actions nor our words will ever force God to consider us. Instead, His perfect love is the reason for His intervention in our lives. As Christians, whenever we pray, we are communicating with our real Father. We are responding to a relationship—not a tradition or religious practice. Like our search for holiness, prayer, too, involves an intimate relationship with God.

> *Neither our actions nor our words will ever force God to consider us. Instead, His perfect love is the reason for His intervention in our lives.*

Even when we understand that prayer is inseparably linked to a relationship with God, we still complicate matters by assuming that prayer is something we do. We will find though, if we just do prayer, we go through the motions but end up avoiding an intimate relationship with God. The goal is to be in prayer and to welcome that close relationship with Him.

When I was the pastor of my first congregation in Princeton, Indiana, there was a man who always brought his sons to worship with him. Their mother never came. I often wondered why she did not attend with her family. When I asked the father about it, he said, "She just seems to want to stay home." Well, I decided to pay her a visit and personally invite her to the church. Driving to her house, I thought through some encouraging and motivating words I would say to her. I knocked on her door and when she answered, introduced myself. "Hi! I'm Reverend Hunter from the church that your husband and boys attend." She cheerfully invited me to come inside.

From the moment I hit the threshold until ninety minutes later, that woman never shut up—I mean never! I kept waiting for her to take a breath. I am not sure if she ever did. She must have been breathing from her ears or through her skin or something. She talked and talked while I sat on the couch thinking, "This is the loneliest woman I have ever seen in my life. She wants so desperately to have a relationship with somebody. Why hasn't she been to church?" I simply did not understand. Finally, after all of my previous efforts had failed, I stood up and slowly backed my way toward the door. "I really have to go," I said. I am sure she kept talking as I closed the door.

Later, I met with an older pastor who was a counselor-type. I described my encounter with the lady and explained how much she craved closeness with another person. The pastor looked up at me and shook his head. "You don't get it, do you?" he said. "She wasn't trying to be intimate. By talking all the time, she was keeping her distance and keeping the floor. She was seizing control. By talking, she did not have to open herself up to you as you asked her questions. She didn't have to give you anything she didn't want to give you. That lady wasn't looking for intimacy—she was avoiding it."

Whenever we launch into long prayer times with God, filling the silence with creative and persuasive words, we are doing the same thing with Him—avoiding a deep relationship, dodging His questions, and ignoring His voice. When the Apostle Paul said in 1 Thessalonians 5:17, "Pray without ceasing," he was not referring to the quantity of words we use or the length of our prayers. Instead, he was referring to the frequency of our communication with God—to the opportunities we take to be with Him. Those opportunities usually consist of brief prayers. Only our intimate relationship with God, not the quantity of our words, makes our prayers effective.

> *Only our intimate relationship with God, not the quantity of our words, makes our prayers effective.*

Still, offering our prayers and then completely trusting God with them is a considerable challenge for us. We tend to act as if God does not fully understand what is best for us and perhaps even more amazing than that, assume that we do! This sloppy theology leads us to pray the answers. That is, we fervently pray our lengthy prayers—persevering until we come up with what we think are good answers to them. The personal brainstorming sessions all but leave God out of the picture. God's answers to our prayers are so much better than our own personal solutions. He is aware of every single aspect of our situations including what they were, what they are, and what they will be in the future.

Due to original sin, we are often unable to completely calculate or understand God's answers. We have an inability to always know the correct answer to our prayers, but I believe we can adopt the correct concept of prayer.

Recently, there was an article in a scientific journal about a man who had a hematoma on the left hemisphere of his brain.

It had caused significant brain damage. When the neuro-psychologist examined him, he asked the man some mathematical questions. When asked, "What is 2 + 2?" The man responded, "3." The doctor became very excited. In fact, he was thrilled. I read further—mainly to understand why he was thrilled that 2 + 2 = 3. I realized that the doctor saw what I did not see. He observed that the man had not said forty nine or anything really ridiculous. While it was obvious that he could no longer calculate, he still had the ability to approximate. To the doctor, that was immensely important. Further questions revealed the same truth. When asked how many days were in a year, the man said, "three hundred." When asked if fourteen children would make a family or a school, he responded, "Fourteen children is too many for a family but too few for a school."

While we may not know God's answers to our prayers, we can approximate. As I pray I often include, from my limited understanding, my idea of God's perfect answers, but I keep in mind that His answers may be different from my requested ones. Beyond that, it is obvious that sometimes God chooses to use prayer on the spot and other times He has a different plan. Even though His plan may seem confusing or painful to us, we know that He answers our prayers just as He wants—in His perfect way and in His perfect timing.

For instance, one of my sons has an asthma problem. As a young boy, he would often wake up in the middle of the night barely able to breathe. Every time it happened, Becky and I would do the same things. We would hurry into his room, lay our hands on him, and pray for immediate physical healing. Sometimes, God would respond to that very specific request and our son would breathe freely. Other times, we had to give him additional medication and carry him into the bathroom where we turned on the shower's hot water and waited until the steam helped him breathe better. Occasionally, though, we were forced to rush him to the hospital. We had prayed the same prayer every time. So, why the difference in the responses? We have no idea!

Jesus instructs us to pray simply. We are to listen for God and express what is on our hearts. Regardless of our trials and His responses to our prayers, He weeps for us in our pain and loves us too much not to allow growth in our lives. In Matthew 6, Jesus provided us with His prayer—the LORD's Prayer. It is our model. As Jesus said, we must learn to "pray, then, in this way:"

The LORD's Prayer

Our Father who art in heaven,
Hallowed be Thy name.
Thy kingdom come.
Thy will be done,

On earth as it is in heaven.
Give us this day our daily bread.
And forgive us our debts, as we also have forgiven our debtors.
And do not lead us into temptation, but deliver us from evil.
For Thine is the kingdom, and the power, and the glory, forever.
Amen. (Matthew 6:9–13)

The LORD's Prayer is the ideal example for us. It demonstrates the form our prayers should take. By reflecting on the prayer of Jesus, we can increase our understanding of God, His sovereignty, and our position as His children. For the remainder of the chapter, we will concentrate on the three primary components of the LORD's Prayer—all of which He wanted us to include in our prayers.

The first component has to do with recognizing the holiness of God. This should always be the initial ingredient in prayer. The first few words of the LORD's Prayer establish an incredible connection: "Our Father, who art in heaven, Hallowed be Thy name." What a vast contrast: Our Father—so close, Who art in heaven—so far. Hallowed be Thy name—sacred, honored, and untouchable. These contrasting elements are also the basis of our hope.

For instance, we all are aware that God is everyone's Creator. He is the all-powerful, all-knowing, Creator God who knit each of us together in our mother's womb. However,

> *Even though His plan may seem confusing or painful to us, we know that He answers our prayers just as He wants—in His perfect way and in His perfect timing.*

once we become Christians, our primary connection with Him is no longer simply as man to Maker. In Romans 8:15, Paul said, "For you have not received a spirit of slavery leading to fear again, but you have received a spirit of adoption as sons by which we cry out, 'Abba! Father!'" Notice the unique connection we have with God when we believe in Jesus Christ. The word "Abba" actually means "Daddy"—the word a child uses to call his father.

There is a stark difference between those of us who know God simply as Maker and those of us who know Him as Father. Through Jesus Christ, every one of us is invited to have a personal relationship with God. Romans 10:9 tells us, "That if you confess with your mouth, 'Jesus is LORD,' and believe in your heart that God raised Him from the dead, you will be saved." A wonderful and mysterious union with the "hallowed" God is available to us.

There is a stark difference between those of us who know God simply as Maker and those of us who know Him as Father. Through Jesus Christ, every one of us is invited to have a personal relationship with God.

Greg Norman, an outstanding Australian golfer, was raised in a very disciplined household. His father was not an affectionate or loving man, but very stern. As a child, many times Greg longed to hug his father after he had been away on a business trip, but knew that he was not the type of man he could freely run up and hug. Instead, from as far back as he could remember, his father would greet him by shaking hands.

In the 1996 Master's tournament, Greg was leading by seven or eight strokes. In the last round, he blew the lead when Nick Faldo sank a birdie on the last putt and won the tournament. As the two men approached each other, Greg tried to smile. He walked up to Nick and stuck out his hand. Well, Nick Faldo is a very "huggy" guy. And so, instead of shaking hands with Greg, he just hugged him. For some time, they both stood there hugging each other and smiling. By the time they were finished, Greg was sobbing and wiping his eyes. The next day, an interviewer asked Greg, "Why were you crying—because you lost the tournament?" Greg smiled and said, "No. I've lost a lot of tournaments. I'll lose a lot more. I was crying because I had never been hugged like that by another man before."

As human beings, there is something we need, not only to live abundant lives, but also even to survive. It is not discipline, accountability, justice, or even wisdom. It is love. God's love changes our perspective of Him, the world, and ourselves. There are many of us who attempt to pull God closer by bringing Him lower to meet our own understanding. In the process, we ignore His holiness and transcendence—both very important aspects of God. The truth is, we cannot get closer to God, or to other people for that matter, by forming an inaccurate opinion about them. Relationships based on misconceptions, if such relationships do exist, are artificial. In other words, if we are going to really love God, we need to get to know Him. And, the point remains the same concerning our relationships with other people.

Effective love and closeness stem from focusing on the others not on ourselves. Most of us love in terms of who we are and then wonder why we do not have any relational successes. Those who love effectively will always love on the basis of others' natures. Therefore, it is very important to understand that when we say to God, "Hallowed be Thy name," we are connecting to Him in accordance with His nature and love, not our own. God is our Father in heaven and He loves us more than we can imagine, but His standards never change. He is high and lifted up. So, a large part of prayer is seeking to know Him for who He really is.

Then Jesus prayed, "Thy kingdom come, Thy will be done on earth as it is in heaven." Obviously, there is a difference between what is done in heaven and what is done on earth. In heaven, God's holiness is pure and unadulterated. On earth it can be hard to see His will being accomplished.

Achieving victory over sin involves more than accountability, Scripture memory, or a resolute character.

In an attempt to make His will happen on earth, the church continually creates more moral rules. Then it finds abounding frustration when it tries to hold everyone accountable to the rules it creates. To some extent, creating rules is a normal reaction. We live in a country of regulations. In fact, in Washington D.C., there is a book consisting of 130,000 pages of federal regulations. The ironic twist is that although we have regulations for nearly anything imaginable, our world is still falling apart.

The reason for that is that doing God's will is more than obeying a command or adhering to a regulation. Achieving victory over sin involves more than accountability, Scripture memory, or a resolute character. God's will being done on earth primarily involves God's movement in our lives and our love for Him. The point is addressed well in this story:

There once was a boy who left his father in order to attend a school far away from home. He regretted having to go, but his father, who was very wealthy, encouraged him to pursue the best education possible. So, living in another country with his relatives, he studied hard and excelled but was unable to see his father for many years. In time, the father died. News spread throughout the community that his son was the sole inheritor of the man's fortune. Once word reached the son, he returned to his father's house, but so did two imposters trying to claim his fortune.

Since the son had been away for many years no one recognized him. The executor of the estate remembered that the true son was an incredible archer. So, he said, "Here's what I will do. At the other end of this field, I will place a picture. All of you must try to hit it in the center." Then, taking a portrait of the father, he placed it on the ground as the target. The first archer stepped forward, aimed at the portrait, and hit the picture directly in the center. The second archer also hit the picture in the center. But the third archer never even raised his bow. Instead, he broke down and wept saying, "I cannot shoot at a portrait of my own father." The true son would never dream of hurting the memory of his father.

We as Christians should feel the same way about our heavenly Father. We should yearn for His will to be done on earth as it is in heaven. We should love Him so deeply that we would never dream of hurting Him. When we value our relationship with Him, treasure His love for us, and honor His holiness, His will is done on earth and in our lives. On earth, doing God's will should not be about simply quitting the bad stuff. It is about allowing God to fill us so completely with His love that we dwell on the joy of loving Him.

The second component of the LORD's Prayer involves voicing our physical, emotional, and spiritual needs to God. As we lay our needs before Him, we eventually become more aware of the beauty of God's timing. Remember that He does not wonder what our needs are. The Bible says that He knows what our needs are before we ever ask. He wants to hear us because He is more concerned about being our Father than He is about granting our requests. Providing us with good gifts is a natural and wonderful aspect of God's character, but that is not His primary focus.

> *On earth, doing God's will should not be about simply quitting the bad stuff. It is about allowing God to fill us so completely with His love that we dwell on the joy of loving Him.*

When we pray, "Give us this day our daily bread," God is granting us another reason to come to Him and deepen the relationship. We may not view our needs in that manner, but God uses our needs to draw us nearer to Him. Physically, financially, or emotionally—most of us could not go a week or even a day without God's provision for us in any one of these areas. His provision in the midst of our poverty forces us to become acutely aware of His presence. Those of us who live in need, experience the profound blessing of His faithfulness.

Those of us who are abundantly provided for in this life, have the wonderful honor and responsibility to abundantly give.

Those of us who are abundantly provided for in this life, have the wonderful honor and responsibility to abundantly give.

There is a story about a little boy who was walking along a dark road with his father one night. They were headed up the narrow passage that led to their farmhouse several miles away. The boy, who was about five years old, could only see about two feet ahead because the only light they had was a lantern that his father was carrying. The boy kept envisioning all of the wild animals that could spring out of the dark and devour them. As they quietly padded up the road, he became more and more scared. Straining his eyes, he searched desperately for the farmhouse but could only see darkness. Finally, he looked at his father and cried, "Dad. I am so scared. It's so dark! And the light doesn't reach very far." The father smiled down at him and said, "That seems true right now. But if we just keep walking, we'll find out that the light reaches all the way to the end of the road."

For those of us who just have a little bit of God's provision, it is easy to get panicked because we cannot see the end of the road. Still, our Father says the same thing to us. He tells us to just keep walking and assures us that He will provide as much as we need to take the next step. Eventually, we will learn that His light reaches all the way to the end. The Bible says, "Thy word is a lamp to my feet and a light to my path" (Psalm 119:105). It does not say that it is a "headlight" toward our goal. The only thing required of us is to take each obvious next step.

> ## *The only thing required of us is to take each obvious next step.*

In addition to our apparent needs, we also have a less obvious, but a significant spiritual need—forgiveness. The LORD's prayer teaches us that we must always remember what God did for us. He forgave us, despite the fact that we were the ones who owed Him. When we read "And forgive us our debts, as we also have forgiven our debtors," it communicates the fact that we owed God. Through Jesus Christ the price for each Christian's debt to God was paid. Our gratefulness for that can and should be reflected in how we respond to others— we must forgive them. One story passed down through the centuries illustrates this point well:

When Leonardo da Vinci was painting the Last Supper he became involved in a terrible dispute with a man in town. After the quarrel, he angrily painted the man's face into the face of Judas. For years to come he wanted everyone, even people who did not know the man, to look at that face and hate it. Yet as he turned to paint the face of Christ, he found that after hours, days, and weeks, he could not picture it. He knew what the problem was. Resolutely, he stepped back to the face of Judas and painted over his enemy's face, forgave him, and then returned to the face of Christ. By forgiving the man, da Vinci was able to accept God's forgiveness and move on. The face of Christ that we now admire in the Last Supper painting is the product of Leonardo's forgiveness.

Many of us wonder from time to time why we do not feel closer to God; the reason may be a non-forgiving attitude. Coming to grips with our own propensity to harm others, our own sinful nature, and God's abundant mercy can provide us with the understanding and grace to forgive. Keep in mind that forgiveness is a lot like healing. Sometimes, God heals us immediately. Other times, healing takes time. The same is true for forgiveness. There are times when we will feel absolute relief when we forgive. Other times we will have to remind ourselves that we have forgiven. The fact that we struggle with keeping our forgiveness alive reflects our desperate need for God. He wants us to yield to Him and allow Him to work in our hearts.

The third and final part of the LORD's Prayer involves understanding that life is an ongoing battle. Not only are we "not in Kansas anymore," we are not in Oz, and we are surely not in Eden. Many of us believe that if we simply accept Christ all of our troubles will go away. We may believe that depression, financial hardship, relational difficulties, physical ailments, and even personality differences just evaporate. They do not. We only have the final victory and healing in heaven. On earth, we have it dispensed in bits.

Jesus finished the LORD's Prayer with these words, "And do not lead us into temptation, but deliver us from evil. For Thine is the kingdom, and the power, and the glory, forever." Jesus said that there will be times when we experience temptation because there will be times when we face testing. Therefore, what we need to do each day is ask for the deliverance of God.

I think that all of us, in our natural minds, want to come to a place in life where we can coast—where we can say, "This is the place where everything is going to be all right." But it will never happen. Life is challenging all the way along. That is by design. We need God every day and every hour.

Fortunately, God has chosen not to build weak people. He has chosen to build strong champions. And He knows how to do it in us. The fact is, when He chooses us to bless others, it does not mean it will be easy to accomplish. We do not easily become strong. We only become strong by testing. The exciting part is that God will deliver us. So, when we do experience horrific times, we must depend on the promise of God:

> Even to your old age and gray hairs, I am He; I am He who will sustain you. I have made you and I will carry you; I will sustain you, and I will rescue you. (Isaiah 46:4 NIV)

What a wonderful promise! When experiencing bad times, we can say, "This too shall pass—God promised."

Our main job is simply to get up in the morning and get going. It is not about trying harder; it is about letting God work. It is not about working harder; it is about showing up. It is about putting one foot in front of the other. It is about believing in the faithfulness of God and persevering. We cannot deliver ourselves through our own hard work and deeds. We are not the ones overcoming the odds and achieving victory. God is doing that through us. He is the one Who delivers us from evil. We are in His kingdom—it is by His power and to His glory that He frees us.

We can begin to appreciate the unique and wonderful relationship we have with God by praying in the manner of the LORD's Prayer. Prayer is powerful and effective. Our needs draw us closer to Him, our paid debts make us grateful to

Him, and our available escapes from evil cause us to offer Him our praises. As we continue the Christian walk, may we all seek to pray in the manner of the LORD.

Profits of Holiness

"How little people know who think that holiness is dull.
When one meets the real thing, it is irresistible."

—C.S. Lewis, *Letters to an American Lady*

*W*hen I counsel couples before they marry, I inform them that many of their future discussions will revolve around two major issues. First, if they plan to have children, they will spend a large part of their lives talking about kids, caring for them, and praying for them. Second, almost every day of their marriage, they will talk about finances. In fact, a good portion of their conflicts will stem from the topic of money.

In the parable of the talents (Matthew 25:14-30), Jesus pointed out the importance of responsible and wise management of possessions. As Christians, we must strive to be faithful stewards. Still, the Bible reveals something more substantial than the frugal management and lifelong enjoyment of material wealth. God's desire for us is to acquire true wealth. That is more important than accumulating material riches because it is eternal and intimately linked to our relationship with God. Our abundant material possessions can even hinder our acquisition of true wealth. Living without some of our "stuff" may actually make our lives much richer.

At the Sermon on the Mount, Jesus said:

> Do not lay up for yourselves treasures upon earth, where moth and rust destroy, and where thieves break in and steal. But lay up for yourselves treasures in heaven, where neither moth nor rust destroys, and where thieves do not break in or steal; for where your treasure is, there will your heart be also. (Matthew 6:19-21)

In these verses, Jesus was pointing us toward the true riches of heaven. It is a wealth that we can enjoy for eternity. As the faithful Shepherd, Jesus guides us away from our human and often misdirected concepts of wealth toward a true treasure.

Jesus was not implying that possessing material wealth is inherently evil. Often, people who believe that the Bible opposes material wealth cite a popular but misquoted verse: "Money is the root of all evil." The truth is, God is the One who blesses us with material gifts. The actual verse in I Timothy 6:10 says, "For the love of money is a root of all sorts of evil."

So there is nothing wrong with having possessions. In fact, God has given all of us some material goods for our enjoyment—and ultimately, for our praise to Him. However, the type of wealth we seek exposes what is in our hearts. Even though having worldly possessions is not evil in and of itself, our shoddy management of them, along with our failure to understand their effect on our lives, can lead us into all sorts of snares. Chasing after the accumulation of wealth steals us away from reliance on God. In turn, our lives can be filled with many pains. When we store up worldly treasures or pursue them with a burning desire, we fail to recognize just how much they cost us. Our wealth is not the real problem. It is, instead, great love for wealth that costs us so dearly.

We need to ask ourselves these questions:

- How much of what we own owns us?
- What treasures of God are we sacrificing for the wealth of the world?
- How often do those things take us away from what is truly important?
- What can we do without, and are we willing to do without it?

The following verse is an encouragement to us, especially when we know that God will help us lay aside anything that is a hindrance to growing in holiness:

> Therefore, since we have so great a cloud of witnesses surrounding us, let us also lay aside every encumbrance, and the sin which so easily entangles us, and let us run with endurance the race that is set before us. (Hebrews 12:1)

The blessings of material wealth are not heaven bound. In fact, if we are not careful, they can become encumbrances in our pursuit of God. Although they will perish in time, they are still powerful enough to prevent us from accumulating the true wealth of God. But as we yield to God we will discover that the treasures to die for are His heavenly blessings.

Give Me Some Credit!

In these days, most of us do a great deal of our financing by credit card. More so than ever, we hold to the notion, "Buy now; pay later!" Whether we are buying a car or house, eating out, or shopping, we tend to feel as if we need it now. So we buy it—on credit. Currently, as American consumers, we already owe 89 percent of all the money we make to creditors! That means, only 11 percent of all of our money is disposable income (money that is not owed to anyone). Now, there is nothing wrong with having credit cards—if we can pay them off. Nevertheless, credit cards can be tremendous temptations for us and the creditors know it. The other day I was at the mall. (No, I was not selling snow cones this time!) The stores were doing a big promotion for a Mall Card. Posted signs indicated that by getting one of these cards, it was possible to receive 2 percent back on every purchase. "Wonderful," I thought. "We can all get rich!" I did some quick calculations in my head. If I were to spend $100, then I can get $2 back. If I spend $1000, I can make $20. And if I spend $10,000, I can get back $200! What a deal!

I picked up some information on it. As I read the Mall Card pamphlet, I noticed something shocking. As usual, for the first six months they offered a compelling introductory interest rate. However, after the first six months the rules change—drastically. A cash advance is charged 2.5 percent interest and $3.50 per transaction is charged to the account. Failure to pay on time equates to a $20 late fee added to the bill. And once the introductory time expires, the interest rate rockets to 21.4 percent. I thought, "This thing is unbelievable!" And to top it all off, the slogan printed on the front of the card read, "Shopping is its own reward!" Its own reward? It is its own punishment unless we can pay it off every time. I did not get the card. In fact, I plan never to get another credit card even though, like most Americans, I receive daily offers for a new one.

The Mall Card story illustrates an important point. The immense cost of material wealth comes in the maintenance. Our worldly possessions continue to drain us even after we obtain them, and we often do not realize the bondage they create. Think about it! What do those who are rich stand to lose? Everything, because there are more responsibilities, more maintenance, and more things to protect. Conversely, those who are poor stand to lose nothing because energy and time can be directed toward different treasures. Those of us who treasure our wealth are bound to the practice of maintaining it. It can even force us to sacrifice the things we love (our family, our friends, our relationship with God, and even our morals). And when we sacrifice those things for wealth, we lose. We have a choice to make—the adoration of our wealth or our growing intimacy with God.

"Every good thing bestowed and every perfect gift is from above" (James 1:17)

Remember Abram? When God called him, He said, "Go forth from your country." God asked him to leave everything behind for the sake of Him. In essence, He told him if he wanted to live in the Promised Land (a perfect land), he must leave the land he was now in right now—he must forsake the material things he treasured. Remember Moses? To Moses, God made it clear that if he wanted to lead His children to the Promised Land and have perfect freedom for everybody, he must give up the treasures of Egypt. If Abram had chosen to remain in his homeland, he would have lost the treasures of the promised land for His people. If Moses and the Israelites had decided not to leave Egypt they, too, would have lost the promised land of God. The lesson here is that before we can have the best, there must be a curtailing of the least. In order to have what is perfect we must leave behind what is good. All the material things we have in our lives are good. "Every good thing bestowed and every perfect gift is from above" (James 1:17). These gifts are for us to use and enjoy. They are even more specifically for the use of God's kingdom. So we are not talking about giving up everything to live in abject poverty. We are talking about priorities. We are talking about the matters of our hearts because if we are not careful, if we are not focused on God, we will take those gifts and change them into idols—idols that can steal life away from us.

In the early 1900s, the Alaskan Klondike was filled with pockets of gold mines. By the thousands, teams of people poured into the area digging for gold and hoping to strike it rich. Most of the gold had been removed within a few years. Still, many of the people remained after the gold rush and eventually made Alaska their home. Not long ago, some people were exploring the Klondike when they discovered a little cabin. Upon entering, they saw a huge pile of gold resting on a table. Nearby, two human skeletons were lying on the floor. As they approached the table, one of them noticed a letter neatly folded on top of the gold. It read: "We discovered a wonderful mine. We mined more and more gold everyday, but we forgot about the winter. A storm came up suddenly. It's been storming for days. We won't get out of here." The two men had amassed a tremendous amount of gold, but they eventually starved to death because they had forgotten about the winter. The desire for wealth not only clouded their thinking, but it also cost them their lives.

If we love money, it will cost us, too. If our minds are filled with ways to increase our wealth there will be little room for thoughts of how to please God. If we attempt to fill our homes and hearts with adorning treasures, we will end up trapped inside by our own greed and fears. True wealth, though, is freeing. True wealth focuses our attention and energy on what is of eternal importance.

Super Simple

A few years ago, Becky and I knew we would be entering a prolonged, difficult, financial period. We had joyfully and willingly placed ourselves under some important financial obligations that would affect us for years to come. So, we made the decision to live on a very tight budget. When we did that, we sold our house and moved into an apartment—neither gated nor fancy—just an apartment. It was not a stressful move. In fact, we found living there to be less stressful than living in a house.

Seriously, when the refrigerator breaks down I just call up the management and say: "Your refrigerator broke down." When the heat is not working properly they answer the phone in the complex's business office and I say, "I know you would want to know that your furnace is not working properly." The yard work gets done while I am working at church and our roof (which is the floor of the apartment above us) never leaks. The fact is that it is absolute freedom for my family and me to live where we do. However—please hear me—it is not more or less holy to live in an apartment than it is to live in a house. This is about trying to live a simpler life. It is about both what we can do without and what has the potential to steal us away from the true purposes of God

My once new jeep, now a run-down, beat-up, old, 100 and some-odd thousand miles, ragtop vehicle without air conditioning, helps to make the point, too. There is no special virtue in driving an old car like that rather than a new car. And there is certainly no virtue in owning a car without air rather than owning one with air. In fact, that is just stupidity when you live in Florida, but I bought the car when I first moved down here from up north. When the salesman asked me, "Do you want air?" I said, "Nah, its a convertible. If it gets hot, I'll just take the top down."

Little did I know about Florida heat. To experience its intensity without ever leaving the comfort of home, just throw open the door of a dishwasher at the conclusion of the hot rinse cycle. The heat and humidity are identical to those of an Orlando summer day—but I digress. The point is this; because I have a rickety and junky car, I do not worry about my car. I could leave the keys in it and nobody would steal it. I am not the slightest bit concerned about it being stolen, scratched, or dented. My car is not one of my concerns. Living simply, I can spend my energy on what is truly important— God and people.

> *When we choose to live a simpler life, we find freedom.*

Jesus described in Mark 4:19, our tendency to allow "the worries of the world and the deceitfulness of riches and the desires for other things" to choke us and make us unfruitful. As a nation that takes pride in wealth we believe that our riches will satisfy us, but instead they cost us dearly—robbing us of time and focus. When we choose to live a simpler life, we find freedom. In addition, when we use our riches to glorify God's kingdom, we are released from the strong pull of lust and greed. It is important that we consider what to rid our lives of to make us freer and to make our lives simpler. Life does not have to be filled with urgency, pursuit, and constant competition. God can make our lives fruitful even without our striving— even in our simplicity.

Consider the ultimate destiny of all material things. Their destiny will always be death and destruction and personal awareness of that can prevent us from wasting a lot of time and energy. The physical world around us is dying even as we go about our daily business. Food molds, garments wear out, fields are overgrown with weeds, precious possessions tarnish, and our bodies fall apart.

A few days ago, I was at the gym. As I was working out, I looked up and saw an old guy in the mirror looking back at me. I am not sure where he came from—but he looked very familiar. When I moved, he moved. When I blinked, he blinked. For a long time, we stared at each other and wondered where the years had gone. The truth is, I am at the gym almost every day. I work out like crazy. I run, lift weights, and even do the stair-master thing. But no matter how hard I work my body, gravity wins. As a younger man, I used to work out to look better. Now that I am 50, I work out so that I do not look as bad as I would if I did not. Notice the subtle shift? At my age, when I look down at the mirror, my head stops, but my face keeps going. That is not a good thing. Still, it is natural.

Ecclesiastes 12 gives us a wonderful illustration of aging. While it may seem dismal, it is reality. The flip-side is that it can encourage us to remember God and hold fast to His unchanging Spirit. The Bible teaches us that even though we are falling apart, we need not lose heart. "Though our outer man is decaying, yet our inner man is being renewed day by day" (2 Corinthians 4:16b). More than ever, we have to realize that material pleasures and wealth turn to dust. And in light of eternity, they cannot save us. However, there are eternal treasures available to us that we can accumulate. They are treasures that will never decay. Even while our bodies are growing old, we can invest in the treasures of God and experience them to the fullest when we are called home.

A Treasure Beyond Measure

A long time ago, I heard a story about a preacher who had been invited to a rich Texan's ranch. The man owned a great deal of land. It stretched for miles and miles all around his beautiful ranch-style home. Rather quickly, the preacher discerned that the Texan was extremely proud of what he had accomplished in his life. After eating an extravagant supper, the man escorted the preacher to a patio that was situated on top of his house. Gazing toward the setting sun, he placed his arm around the preacher and said, "You know, I started out with nothing. But I want you to look over here." He motioned to the north. "Everything you see in that direction, I own." He then turned him another 90 degrees and said, "Everything you see in this direction, I own." And then he turned him another 90 degrees and said, "Everything you see in that direction, I own." Finally, they were facing west again and he repeated, "And everything you see in this direction, I own." The man seemed truly satisfied with his success as he smiled and surveyed his awesome possession.

Then, the preacher turned to him and said, "Well Ralph, I'm glad for you." He placed a kind arm around the rich Texan and pointed up, "My question for you is this: How much do you own in that direction?"

That is the exact question Jesus would ask us. How much do we own in the direction of heaven? In this life, Jesus wants us to do what matters. And what matters is what affects the eternal. Even when we are blessed with material wealth, it will never be enough. God wants us to accumulate an enduring wealth that lasts for eternity. But we must be able to recognize the difference between what He gives us to be delighted in for a short time and what He gives us to be delighted with for an eternity. In other words, there is a distinction between our playthings of earth and the treasures of God. It is important that we do not confuse them.

> *In other words, there is a distinction between our playthings of earth and the treasures of God.*

We need to understand what Jesus said when he admonished, "Lay up for yourselves treasures in heaven" (Matthew 6:19). In the Greek, the verb tense and mood involves a continuous and repeated action. It is not a one-time thing. It was also an instruction to us rather than a request. That is why we should never feel greedy about wanting heavenly treasures. It is not about gathering selfishly, but following the commandments of God. God wants us to pursue Him and His treasures. He wants to share His wealth.

Before we came to Christ we were in debt. In fact, according to Romans 2:5, we were storing up wrath for ourselves—like a credit card stores up debt. However, when we came to Christ, the balance sheet shifted. We were no longer in debt because all of our debt became paid in Christ. He paid off all of it. Now, as Christians, we have an account in heaven where we can lay up treasures. Our good works and our intimate relationship with Him increase those treasures. Yet even before we ever did our first good work, we had heavenly benefits in Christ. Ephesians 1 says specifically that we are already rich in Christ just from what He has given us. We have answered prayer (Matthew 7:7). We have all of heaven, eternity, and our citizenship there (Luke 10:20). We have peace (John 14:27). We have joy that surpasses understanding (John 15:11). We have victory in every case of spiritual overcoming (John 16:33). We have much more by simply coming into a relationship with Christ. But added to that, we also have an open account in heaven in which to place our treasures. In ways we cannot fathom, somehow, the good works we do in Christ multiply the benefits we will receive in heaven.

Often, the act of being faithful in good works is what God uses to change our hearts.

Throughout Scripture we are provided with many illustrations of how to obtain these treasures. The exciting part is that not only will we receive these treasures when we enter heaven, but we also experience the positive impact they have on us while we are on earth. Remember that we will never become holy or accumulate treasures by simply doing things—by jumping through the "hoops," so to speak. Instead, developing intimacy with God is what changes us. As we draw closer to Him, our behaviors shift as our motivations for doing those behaviors change.

God's treasures are not gained by our pursuits, but as by-products of our relationship with Him. In a way, His treasures naturally accumulate as He draws us nearer to Him and as we seek to love Him more. So laying up treasures in heaven involves our desires, behaviors, goals, and motivations reflecting the transforming work that He is performing in us.

At the same time, this does not mean that we should give up doing good works because we do not feel completely holy yet, or because our motivations are not absolutely pure. Instead, we must act in faith and ask God to work through us even when we do not feel perfect, adequate, or strong enough. Often, the act of being faithful in good works is what God uses to change our hearts.

The Bible explains that throughout our lives there are three major areas where we can lay up the treasures of heaven. First, we can lay up treasures in heaven by the management of our material goods. Second, we can lay up treasures in heaven by the management of our conduct. Finally, we can lay up treasures in heaven by our relationships and investments in people.

Goods for You!

When any of us is great at something, we are great because we took the time to learn the basics. We started out with the basics and built upon them. Everyone, including athletes, musicians, actors, and politicians, all return to the basics whenever there is trouble. The same is true for us in our spiritual lives and in our pursuit of God's treasures.

The first way we can accumulate the treasures of God is by wise management of our material goods. Chapter 3 of the book of Malachi returns us to the basics of capturing this treasure—the basics of the tithe. It says, "Will a man rob God? Yet you are robbing Me?" (v. 8). He continued, "'Test me in this,' said the LORD Almighty, 'and see if I will not throw open the floodgates of heaven and pour out so much blessing that you will not have room enough for it'" (v. 10). This passage is the only one in the Bible in which God said, "Test Me."

God wants us to give, and He desires to reward our faithful giving with blessing beyond measure. He instructed us to give the first 10 percent of everything we get—that is the tithe. A tithe is usually given to the church. Offerings are anything given beyond that amount. It is money that is usually given for something specific. We should strive to use the other 90 percent of our income in responsible ways that have a positive eternal influence on our lives and the lives of others. As we reserve a portion of our income for tithes and offerings to the church (as we faithfully test God) He begins to bless us in various ways. When we give, we are not only setting in motion amazing blessings that will overflow into our lives, but we are involving ourselves in God's work and helping to provide for His people.

> *When we trust God to meet our financial needs, we begin to see Him in more places.*

Like many of us who are believers, I tithe. As a result, I have some remarkable truths to share. When we tithe we are surprised to find how great it feels to go from giving whatever is convenient to giving a full tithe. Secondly, when we trust God with our tithes and offerings, we are amazed at how adequately He answers all of our other needs—and how money is provided. Thirdly, we are pleased with a growing depth in our spiritual life. When we trust God to meet our financial needs, we begin to see Him in more places. And fourthly, we are impressed with how much more important the stewardship of the other 90 percent becomes to us.

Like so many things in the Christian life, tithing has a paradoxical bent—by giving, we receive. By relinquishing a portion of our blessings, we are showered with more blessings from the Giver. Tithing is an immensely rewarding practice. At the same time, it is an integral part of who we are as Christians.

Our tithes and offerings make a difference for Christ in the lives of others. In churches across this country, people accept Jesus Christ into their lives. Every week marriages are put back together. Every week the hungry are clothed and fed—and the list goes on and on. Through our giving, God uses our money, time, and service to change people whom we may not even know. We actually are participating in the work of God for eternity through our benevolence. That is the ultimate and primary reason why we should give. In a culture where money and possessions are practically worshiped, tithing is a powerful step of faith and an effective way to force our spirits to rely on God and God alone.

Conduct Yourselves

Another way to lay up treasures in heaven is through proper management of our conduct. Somebody once said that 90 percent of life is just showing up. To some extent, that is true of Christianity. Christianity involves getting our bodies in the right places—showing up to work, to volunteer, to minister, to listen, to encourage, to support, or to be another warm body. Maturity comes from placing ourselves in the right places, doing what God desires, and being willing to learn and grow. In fact, one of the primary goals of the church is:

...to prepare God's people for works of service, so that the body of Christ may be built up until we all reach unity in the faith and in the knowledge of the Son of God and become mature attaining to the whole measure of the fullness of Christ. (Ephesians 4:12-13)

In order to grow in Christ and experience abundant living, at times we must push our stubborn bodies and emotions to respond to the Spirit of God inside of us. Managing our conduct in a godly way will hurt sometimes, but it has positive results in the end. Many of us, for example, have had Sundays like this:

The alarm clock buzzes; your eyelids struggle to open. You feel as if you had just fallen asleep. After several failed attempts, you force yourself to get up. When your feet hit the floor, you suddenly become aware of the time. You are three snoozes behind schedule. Sacrificially, you wake your husband and decide to forfeit washing your hair so that he has time to shower. Rushing to your 2-year-old's room to wake him, you find that he is already awake and has discovered the chocolate pudding in the refrigerator. After that clean up, you make your way to your 8-year-old daughter's room and pray that she is up and dressed—as usual. She is not! She smiles at you sleepily when you turn on the light. Sitting up slowly in her bed and yawning, she begins telling you her long, complicated dream while you sort frantically through her dresses. At that moment, your 6-year-old daughter begins crying. You call for your husband to attend to her. He does not respond. You call again. He still does not answer. By now, you are perturbed. Quickly tossing a dress to your older daughter, you hurry into your other daughter's room, pick her up, and set out to locate your husband who failed to answer you. It turns out he is in the shower – singing "What a Friend We Have in Jesus." By the time the family is in the van, you are fuming, your husband is hurt and somewhat baffled, and your children are either crying or complaining. The thought crosses your mind, "We should just stay home," but you keep it to yourself. You are glad that you do because once you settle down at church, you realize that the sermon, the worship, and the people are just what you all needed. All that was required of you and your husband was to get your bodies there—and God somehow did the rest.

Management of our conduct involves doing what we know is right or best even when we do not feel like it.

Many times, the crux of the Christian life is to honor God by simply showing up—being where He wants us to be. We may not feel like being there, but our feelings are not the most important reference point for our decisions. Management of our conduct involves doing what we know is right or best even when we do not feel like it. Conduct is important. Managing our conduct benefits us as well as others.

The other day, I was talking to somebody who was in a very bad position. He had formed a business partnership with a person who eventually walked out on him. As a Christian, he knew that he was responsible to make good whatever he could, but the financial prospects looked very bad for him. So, I was sympathizing with him and trying to offer some support. At that point, he held up his hand to me and said,

"Oh, they can take everything we own but nothing of what we love." As I walked away from that conversation, I was impressed with a man who had his priorities straight. He knew that he needed to do the right thing even though it hurt. He knew that there was a greater cause than his feelings and even his financial security. I know that God will bless him for it. And He will do the same for us. We are no different than that man. When we honor God by our conduct, He will bless us in unimaginable ways.

True Treasures "To Die For"

The final way we can capture the treasures of God is by pursuing relationships and investing in the lives of people. Whenever we invest our lives into others, regardless of whether or not we see direct results, treasure is laid up for us in heaven. Every time we choose to love people, regardless of their attitudes or reactions, God reserves another treasure for us. Theoretically, investing our lives in others is very simple, rewarding, and appealing. However, when we come right down to it, loving others can be horribly difficult, painful, and even repugnant. At times, people are cantankerous, ornery, and very uncooperative. All of us have these same qualities. Still, there is no doubt that God wants us to love each other anyway.

While the first two ways of accumulating treasures in heaven involve our behaviors and conduct, there is even more to it. For example, we may be able to achieve excellency in handling our finances, giving to the church, and being faithful in all of our purchases, but we can still miss the point. Beyond that, we may be able to attain proficiency in controlling our emotional reactions, keeping a godly attitude, and behaving like good Christians, but we can still fail to grasp the purpose. Our reason for trying to attain the first two treasures is closely linked to the last treasure—investing our lives in people. It is not our skillful management, sparkling demeanor, or faithful behavior that ultimately matters.

Loving others and investing our lives in them springs out of the love we have for God. Attaining the treasures of God is about building loving relationships. After all, God has always been about relationships—beginning in this world with Adam and Eve.

His greatest goal is to be with us.

In the Garden of Eden, after Adam and Eve ate the fruit, they separated themselves from God by hiding themselves from Him. Even today, we do the same thing with Him and others. Our sins cause us to hide in shame. Instead of seeking love, our temptation is to remove ourselves from the very people with whom we ought to become closest. After Adam and Eve sinned and they heard God walking in the garden in the cool of the day, they hid behind a bush. God called out to Adam in Genesis 3:9, "Where are you?" Of course, we know that this is not a question of geography. God knew where he was. It is not like God cannot see behind bushes. Instead, His question was one of biography. He was saying, "Adam, where are you right now?" He wanted Adam to understand that he had separated himself from God—that something horribly significant had happened. At the same time, even though Adam and Eve sinned, even though they had hurt God, He still pursued them. He searched for them because He still loved them. He came to them because He still wanted a relationship.

In Genesis 4:9, there is a similar story. When Cain killed his brother, God came to him and said, "Cain, where is your brother?" God knew where Cain's brother was. He knew what had happened. But instead of wiping Cain off the face of the earth, God came to him. Throughout history, God has always been like this. In fact, His greatest goal is to be with us. Why? Because we are His treasures and He longs for the day when we return home.

Investing our lives in people is complicated and painful. Jesus knew that before He came to earth as a man. He knew the price that He would pay. However, He knew that the significance of His investment would far outweigh the cost. While investing in people is excruciating at times, its rewards are beyond measure.

In *Venus and Mars on a Date,* author John Gray struck the motherload when it comes to pointing out the clinical differences between men and women. He demonstrated just how difficult relationships can be at times. While he criticizes neither sex, he does point to the fact that men and women are constructed differently and therefore communicate differently. Since we communicate differently, intimacy between the two sexes is a much greater challenge than any of us ever imagined.

At one point, John Gray provides a great example. He proposes that most women know that men like to problem-solve and give answers. He points out that a woman will ask a man for advice so that he will talk to her. While he talks, she thinks his words are making him feel closer to her. However, after he talks for quite awhile, she realizes that he is not feeling closer to her—just feeling closer to the subject about which he continues to wax eloquent. On the other hand, a man, if he is polite, will ask a woman to tell him about her day. He will do it in order to get a little bit closer to her. Since women enjoy it when a man expresses this type of interest, she will open up and tell everything—the good parts and the bad parts. The problem is (and the woman does not realize it yet) that a man has incredible difficulty handling the bad parts. Not because it depresses him or worries him, but because he then feels like he must come up with a solution. So he offers ways to fix the bad stuff she told him. However, she was looking to increase intimacy through her information sharing, not to "problem solve." She does not want him to fix it and she lets him know it, too. Startled by her response, he thinks, "Wow! She sure is getting negative." Maybe the smart thing for a man to say is, "Tell me about your day—just the happy parts, please!"

> *We must seek to understand*
> *each other or if that is not*
> *possible, we must seek to*
> *accept our differences.*

John Gray's point is that relationships are complicated but they are not impossible. We must seek to understand each other or if that is not possible, we must seek to accept our differences. Difficulties in communication and diversity in personalities will always produce conflicts. Yet they can be effectively dealt with in a Christ-like manner. Still, it may take time. Even couples who have been married for years experience conflicts and squabbles.

Speaking of marriage, here is a little helpful advice for those of us who are husbands. We are, at some point in time, likely to be confronted with the following question: "You know, if I lost a little weight, I think I'd be a lot more attractive. What do you think?" The silence that follows the question demands a response.

Men, we have just entered into a dimension of time and space where there are no right answers. However, we have got to find one—quickly! And I am here to help. The following are three responses that may sound right to us but they are definitely the wrong things to say.

- **Response Option #1**—"You're perfect for me just like you are!"

  To you this response sounds like an expression of genuine unconditional love does it not? But what your wife heard was, *"You're fat, but I don't mind."*

- **Response Option #2**—"Well, you know you look pretty good to me, but if you want to go on a diet, I'm here to support you. I'll help you. I'll help cook for you. I'll encourage you to exercise. I'll do everything I can to assist you in this thing."

  You think you just expressed support, don't you? But what your wife heard was, *"You're fat and I do mind!"*

- **Response Option #3**—"You know, everybody's so into this weight thing for crying out loud! Everybody's talking about weight, weight, weight! What you weigh doesn't matter, it's about who you are as a person! Weight just doesn't matter!"

  You think you just put things into perspective, don't you? But what your wife heard was, *"You're not only fat, you talk about dumb stuff!"*

The whole issue is very complex. Probably the best thing we can do is to burst into tears and say, "I don't know the right answer, but I love you!" And then crawl out of the room.

The point is, working with each other and relating to each other is very complex even for people who are trying to cooperate. Still, every time we invest our time and lives into another person, we are loving God. Jesus said that in Matthew 25:40. All of those tough people we try to love are Jesus in disguise.

As Christians we should be praying, loving, exercising patience and saying in a hundred ways how important others are to us. What I am talking about is love that suffers long like the love God demonstrated to us. Seeking the treasures of God means loving others as Christ loved us. It means loving God because He paid a dear price for us—His Son. It means allowing Him to fill us so completely that we willingly give portions of our material wealth to Him. We willingly push our bodies and minds into a position to learn and minister, and we willingly suffer for others because we want to love them and love God.

People of Holiness

"It was in this submission of Himself, in which His human will was at one with His divine will, that Christ in His human life realized the perfection of holiness: for Christ was not less holy on earth than He now is in heaven."

—*Father Cuthbert,*
God and the Supernatural

Whoever wants to become great among you must be your servant, and whoever wants to be first must be your slave—just as the Son of Man did not come to be served, but to serve, and to give his life as a ransom for many. (Matthew 20: 26-28)

*A*lthough we may develop in our understanding of what it means to pursue the holiness of God in His strength, we often continue to wrestle with our self-will. Throughout this book, I have repeatedly emphasized a pivotal truth in our pursuit of holiness: the holiness of God cannot be accomplished on our own! To fully experience the joy of His calling and the embracing work of His holiness, we need to grasp this concept. We must surrender to the divine will of God. Otherwise, we will falter and cleave to our infamous "to do" lists for achieving it.

The lists we create, though perhaps impressive in appearance, concentrate primarily on our behaviors and attitudes. Consequently, they fail to acknowledge or esteem our need to submit to the steady, patient, and transforming work of God in our lives. While factual, our "to do" lists fall woefully short of the holiness that God desires. For instance, consider the accurate but misguided "holiness to do" list that I was able to compose from the material in this book:

- live without performing for others or ourselves
- live without anger
- live without lust
- live without worry
- live without seeking revenge or quarrelling
- live in constant fellowship and communication with God
- love others even when we experience intense pain
- give out of our wealth or poverty with a joyful attitude

Does such a list seem unrealistic or impractical and if so, why? It is because the list excludes the primary point of God being the enabler and the only One who can impart holiness, in His timing and in His way. To chase after holiness in our own strength is nothing but ludicrous. It is impossible! While we may be able to portray ourselves as holy to others, inside we are "whitewashed tombs"—dead and fruitless (Matthew 23:27). However, as Christians, we can be hopeful because we know that all things are possible with God (Mark 10:27). Miraculously, the holiness of God is attainable for those of us who surrender to Him. As we aim to maintain our focus on God and allow our lives to yield to His discipline, we experience His steady changing of our lives.

Seeking the holiness of God on a daily basis is far different from most of our presuppositions. Becoming disciplined toward holiness does not demand us to buckle down and try harder. It does not order us to memorize a certain number of verses, pray for a particular length of time, or perform a specific number of good deeds. It does not necessitate that we present ourselves as "squeaky-clean." Instead, when we discipline ourselves unto God and His holiness, we endeavor to remain focused on what is truly important—a personal relationship with our loving God. Every day we surrender to that relationship. Just as being saved requires a deliberate choice, so lifting our eyes to God each day requires a deliberate choice as well. When we welcome God into our lives every day and yield our control to Him, we discipline ourselves and maintain a healthy focus. It is in His strength that we succeed and achieve the great things He has set before us. It is as simple as saying, "Jesus, I can't do this thing on my own. In fact, there is nothing about me that can completely accomplish any of this on my own. I am asking you to work in my life today—to direct me, to move in me, and to change me." Then we must act on the fact that He loves us and will respond accordingly.

Just as being saved requires a deliberate choice, so lifting our eyes to God each day requires a deliberate choice as well.

Many times, I have heard people remark, "It is really narrow thinking to believe that Jesus is the only Way—the only Truth—the only Life! It seems both ignorant and arrogant to assume every person will live forever separated from God unless he or she comes to Him by accepting Jesus Christ as a personal Savior."

I usually respond like this: "We are all in a burning world. In John 10, Jesus said, 'I am the door.' He really is the only way, and that one way is enough. He is the way out of our anger. He is the way out of our confusion. He is the way out of our lust. He is the way out of our pain.

If you were trapped in a burning building, and there was somebody standing by an open door calling you out to safety, would you respond, 'How narrow—what do you mean there is only one way out?' Would you think it is ignorant and arrogant to assume every person in that building must come through that one opening?" Probably not, but we may fail to see the comparison and continue to chase after holiness as if it were attainable without God—as if we could put out the fire of sin on our own. Although we may learn from God's Word, grow from life's experiences, understand through teaching, or imitate the good deeds modeled for us, the full knowledge of the truth escapes our grasp. As Christians we still, at times, think no differently than the world. The world's concept of freedom is being able to make any wrong choice it wants. That is not freedom; that is confusion! In fact, that is danger! However, most of us do end up exploring the fire, touching it, challenging it, and even moving it, but in that process we get burned.

In addition to that, we unwittingly even create traps for ourselves rather than move from the world's temporary satisfactions through the opening Christ offers us. Our self-made traps of pride and selfish ambition become as real as shackles and chains. This world will never satiate our desires. In spite of everything, though, the way to holiness remains through the open door of Christ.

Recognize The Enemy

Jesus said to us:

> Enter by the narrow gate; for the gate is wide, and the way is broad
> that leads to destruction, and many are those who enter it. For the
> gate is small, and the way is narrow that leads to life, and few are
> those who find it. (Matthew 7:13-14)

As we continue our spiritual journey toward holiness, it is
wise to regularly make sure we are still motivated by God
and serving Him. After all, it is not difficult to fall into the
"broad" way of doing things: following our self-will or simply
acquiescing to the plans of others.

In fact, Christ admonished us: "Beware of false prophets,
who come to you in sheep's clothing, but inwardly are ravenous
wolves" (Matthew 7:15). Even within the church, there will
always be, people posed as sheep (followers of Christ) who in
reality are wolves. These people present themselves as devout
Christians, but eventually they may attempt to accomplish
their own selfish ends. True holiness has nothing to do with
selfishness.

Unlike a sheep, a wolf is not a follower at all, but a pursuer—
a predator. A wolf finds fulfillment and peace by devouring
others—by filling himself. It is worth noting that some people
become Christians only because they want to be fulfilled and
experience peace. Christ warned us that there would be those
among us who act like Christians for the sake of self-fulfillment.
However, a Christian is fulfilled and at peace only when he
submits to Jesus Christ and reflects His giving nature. If we are
misguided and behaving "wolf-like" in some areas of life, it is
important to ask God to correct our motivations and goals.

Jesus assured us we would know His sheep:

You will know them by their fruits. Grapes are not gathered from thorn bushes, nor figs from thistles, are they? Even so, every good tree bears good fruit; but the bad tree bears bad fruit. A good tree cannot bear bad fruit, nor can a bad tree produce good fruit. (Matthew 7:16-18)

Only by observing people for a long period of time do we see that it is their lives that offer the evidence we need: words alone are not the verification. As our relationship with God deepens and we begin to mature, it becomes easier to distinguish the good fruit from the bad fruit both in other people and in ourselves. There is nothing refutable about a life lived for Jesus Christ.

A Christian is fulfilled and at peace only when he submits to Jesus Christ and reflects His giving nature.

When I was in seminary, there was a man in my classes who was very skeptical and hostile. His name was Dan. Evidently, Dan had been badly hurt throughout his life because over the years he had developed a bitter and argumentative spirit. Although he was attending seminary, he obviously did not believe in the truth of Jesus Christ. In fact, whenever anybody crossed him, a heated and lengthy debate invariably ensued. Most of the time, Dan ripped the other person's argument and often their confidence to shreds: he was both angry and brilliant.

At the same seminary, there was also a guy named John. He had a sweet, sweet spirit. John was a simple person—a round, red-faced little fellow who had come straight from the farm. He was surprised and humbled that God had called him to pastor a small country church near his home. He was almost equally surprised and humbled that his high school sweetheart (now his wife) was still absolutely crazy about him. By the time I met him, John had been married several years and was the proud father of a couple of kids. The entire family was sweet, little round people. I just loved John!

On one particular day in the seminary cafeteria, John and Dan were sitting at the same table with a group of us. John began expounding on his faith in Jesus—a beautifully simple and honest faith in Christ. Well, this really fired up Dan's engines so after John was finished Dan took him to task. As usual, he raked him up one side and down the other. He took everything John had said and made him look like an absolute fool. Finally, at the end of the chastisement, Dan looked at John and sneered, "John, I wouldn't trade your brain for my dog's brain."

Then, with all the simplicity and love in the world, John looked into Dan's eyes and said, "Ahh, but Dan—I wish you could just have my life. You'd trade lives with me if you could, wouldn't you?" For the first time ever I watched, as Dan became speechless. He just stared silently at John with a blank expression on his face. Then, slowly, tears began to well up in his eyes. Without a word, he grabbed his tray, rose from the table, and walked away. Five years later, Dan committed suicide.

Though a tragic example, it demonstrates that we cannot argue with a life lived for Jesus Christ. We cannot argue with a simple life that is lived out of gratitude for the grace of God—a life that gives itself away continually and voluntarily.

It is not our theological training, good deeds, or cunning wit that changes people, but our changed lives through Christ. There is no refutation of a life like that. Jesus warned us:

> Not everyone who says to Me, "LORD, LORD," will enter the kingdom of heaven; but he who does the will of My Father who is in heaven. Many will say to Me on that day, "LORD, LORD, did we not prophesy in Your name, and in Your name cast out demons, and in Your name perform miracles?" And then I will declare to them, "I never knew you; depart from Me, you who practice lawlessness." (Matthew 7: 21-23)

> ### *Christianity is not about a religion. It is not even about making the world better. It is about a relationship with Christ.*

Sadly, many people believe that doing good deeds, even doing good deeds in the name of Christ, is going to get them into heaven; but they are completely missing the point. The most important aspect of Christianity is the relationship we have with Christ. And that is what we are giving away: the reality of Christ in our lives. Unlike wolves, we have a Shepherd who loves and protects us completely. Christianity is not about a religion. It is not even about making the world better. It is about a relationship with Christ. And until we welcome that relationship, all of our efforts are simply doing things that we want to do.

Hudson Taylor, one of the founders of the modern missionary movement, said this: "If your mother and father, or if your husband and wife, or if your brother and sister, or if your children, or even if your dog is not happier because you've become a Christian, chances are you haven't become a Christian." If you have not become more joyful, giving, loving, patient, gentle, or wise toward others since you have become a Christian, chances are you have missed something crucial.

Quality Sheep

There is a wonderful change that occurs when we choose to believe in Christ and accept Him as our LORD and Savior. First of all, we are automatically granted citizenship in heaven for eternity. Also, we become an active part of the holy family of God. We are beneficiaries of the rewards and treasures that our relationship affords us. However, in addition to the more immediate changes and rewards, there are other character qualities that begin to surface in our lives.

> But we all, with unveiled faces beholding as in a mirror the glory of the LORD, are being transformed into the same image from glory to glory, as from the LORD, the Spirit. (II Corinthians 3:18)

When we become Christians, the Holy Spirit enters our lives and commences His transforming work.

In Matthew 5, Jesus described the character of a maturing Christian—actually, the character of His indwelling Spirit. These character traits are popularly known as the Beatitudes and they represent the inner blessings of God. Bear in mind, the Beatitudes should not be confused with happiness, because happiness is based on circumstances. Instead, the

Beatitudes are the results of His Spirit working in our lives. They are the blessed and developing inner qualities of a believer.

As the people of God, we will naturally manifest these qualities because they are the fruits of our relationship with God. Since we are all unique individuals, the fruit among believers will vary in quantity and quality. Fruit requires time to grow, so we may not experience the fullness of all of the qualities of God until we are in heaven. Each is nonetheless a beautiful attribute of our loving and mighty God. These qualities of God, through Christ, have been imparted to us. And as God's children we must be willing to rearrange and interrupt our lives to allow His character to penetrate our sometimes stubborn, fearful, and angry characters. Daily, Jesus invites us to lay down our burdens and follow Him.

A Look At The Beatitudes

"And opening His mouth He began to teach them, saying, 'Blessed are the poor in spirit, for theirs is the kingdom of heaven'" (Matthew 5:2-3). Those of us who are poor are blessed in that there is a constant dependence on and an awareness of the daily graces of God. On the other hand, those of us who are rich can sometimes miss that blessing. Again, there is nothing wrong with being rich, but it is easy to become misguided into thinking that our daily lives are not dependent upon God's grace. Now, consider what Jesus said in Matthew 5. He took the concept of material wealth and explained it on a spiritual level. "Blessed are those who are poor in spirit," could be translated: blessed are those who realize that they need God in every area of their lives. So, Jesus told us that we are blessed when we realize our inadequacy. We are blessed when we understand that we just cannot quite get things together—when we feel incompetent. We are blessed because our poverty makes us profoundly aware of the truth of our nature. In turn, that has the potential to usher us into an intimate reliance on God.

"Blessed are those who mourn, for they shall be comforted" (Matthew 5:4). To God, expressions of sadness and pain are real and honest responses to trials and hardships. God gave us permission to mourn, to express our pain, and to grieve. It is okay to cry when we suffer. It is normal. However, Jesus referred to a different type of mourning—to something deeper. The mourning He referred to stems not only from personal suffering, but also from our awareness of sin.

There is a sharp contrast between mourning from the pain of a difficult circumstance and mourning over the cause of that painful circumstance. Case in point: whenever our young sons did something wrong, Becky was immediately on top of the situation. Being a good mom meant, at least in part, never letting them get away with anything. While she rarely over-reacted when they did cross the line, justice was delivered swift and sure. Of course, they would cry, mourn, weep, and wail about the unfairness of it all. It was never long though before they would return to her and say, "Mom, I'm so sorry."

Becky would smile, offer a big hug, and ask a very important question: "Are you sorry you did it or are you sorry because you got caught?" There is a huge difference between the two reasons. Many of us are sorry because of the results of our actions. It is rare that we are sorry because we did something wrong.

Jesus admonished all of us to get to the root of the issue— sin is the only valid reason for our sorrow. Jesus said we are blessed when we recognize how our sin has damaged us and caused hurt to God and to those around us. When we mourn over the fact that we will always have the tendency to make mistakes and mess up, we will be comforted and blessed by God.

Then Jesus said this: "Blessed are the gentle (meek), for they shall inherit the earth" (Matthew 5:5). Gentle does not mean weak. In fact, those of us who are gentle are able to remain so because we have an inner strength. We choose to invest energy in what is going to last forever because we love God. We understand that we do not have to run the universe, because God is doing a fine job on His own. We know that we do not have to win every battle, because God has already won the war. We understand that if God is in it, it is going to last and that allows us to be quieter and more joyful. We can simply be gentle.

> *Our challenge is to allow God to fill us so completely that our lives have no room for the artificial replacements of this world.*

Since turning 50, I have realized that I am right at the beginning of old age and I have started to become aware of the blessing in that. Old age is a perfect metaphor for what it means to relinquish control and to concentrate on what is really important. It is a time to decide what is truly significant, what to fight for, and where to invest energy. I, like many of you, know that God will fight the battles and He knows which ones are not worth winning. God will accomplish what He wants to accomplish. "...'Not by might nor by power, but by my Spirit,' says the LORD Almighty" (Zechariah 4:6b NIV).

"Blessed are those who hunger and thirst for righteousness, for they shall be satisfied" (Matthew 5:6). Most of our lives are spent hungering and thirsting after stuff that really does not matter. Most of us live the first part of our lives in fear that we will not fully experience everything in the world. We invest our time and energy chasing after thrills, sensual indulgences, superficial relationships, material gain, perfection, or prestige and significance. Many of us, by the time we reach middle to old age, conclude that those things really do not matter—and that they do not truly satisfy.

Søren Kierkegaard (1813-1855), a Danish philosopher, once said that we can only understand life from backwards to forwards. There is some truth to that, however, we are not limited to that partial truth in our search for satisfaction. Jesus Christ told us that if we want to be truly satisfied we must seek after His righteousness and if we truly do this then we will live satisfied, no matter what our lot in life. He offers us nourishment that sustains both our spirits and our bodies (John 4:32-34). Our challenge is to allow God to fill us so completely that our lives have no room for the artificial replacements of this world.

"Blessed are the merciful, for they shall receive mercy" (Matthew 5:7). In a world that seems to lack mercy, what does it take to be truly merciful? Most importantly, it takes an understanding that God is merciful. He showed us mercy on the cross "…while we were yet sinners He died for us" (Romans 5:8b). Unless we believe in His mercy it will be extremely difficult for us to extend mercy. When we do recognize how good God has been to us, we are able to respond mercifully to others. Beyond that, our mercy is more proactive as in the story of the Good Samaritan. The Samaritan actively demonstrates God's mercy.

True mercy overflows from the gratitude for God that we house in our hearts. We certainly do not have to be called into a worldwide, up-front ministry to communicate God's mercy. Jesus set the example for us when He simply walked along and ministered to those whom He met day after day. As we are filled up with the mercy that God showers down on us, it will naturally spill over into the lives of people we meet along the way.

"Blessed are the pure in heart, for they shall see God" (Matthew 5:8). The pure in heart naturally assume that God has a purpose for every circumstance. The pure in heart can say, "I am glad that I am who I am. I am glad for the rewarding and difficult circumstances in my life because I know that both will draw me closer to God and increase my faith and character."

Being pure in heart does not mean that we never experience a negative or impure thought, although there is more purification as we mature. Even though our lives may seem vastly complicated to us, God is not confused. As the evangelist David Ring puts it, "God never says, 'Oops!'" I like that a lot because it is true that God is waiting for us in every single circumstance. God has not made mistakes in how He has made the world or in how He has made us.

"Blessed are the peacemakers, for they shall be called sons of God" (Matthew 5:9). There are two primary ways this verse can be misinterpreted. The first way results from "peacemakers" sometimes being understood to mean "people who avoid all conflict." That is not the correct definition. Those who avoid all conflict are not peacemakers—cowards, maybe, but not peacemakers. The second misunderstanding is a result of interpreting the verse to mean that striving for peace is a way that we can become children of God. However, there is only one way to become children of God—accept the life that He extended to us in Jesus Christ.

An accurate interpretation of Matthew 5:9 could be summed up in the following way. As we pursue peace and allow God's qualities to fill our lives, we will remind others of God and thereby demonstrate that we are His children. Still, the price of being peacemakers is sacrifice. It may require us to get in the middle of conflicts and perhaps even forego our own safety. It does not mean subduing the parties involved in the conflict through power or intimidation. Peace is not attained in that manner. True peacemakers can see the other people's perspectives. While we are not required to agree, at least we understand their point of view. Jesus was the model peacemaker. While He never sided with sin, He always sided with sinners—including you and me! May we forever continue our journey of faith to be more and more like Him.

Present Holiness

"*Holy has the same root as wholly; it means complete. A man is not complete in spiritual stature if all his mind, heart, soul, strength are not given to God.*"

—*R.J.H. Stewart,*
Spiritual Conferences of 1952

*T*he character of Christ can be a very real presence in our lives as Christians. In Christ, God longs to usher us toward holiness—toward a loving, intimate, and meaningful relationship with Him. However, we live in a world of illusions. The tendency of so many of us is to chase after illusions of holiness. We attempt to look as if we are better than we actually are—to create a more appealing image of ourselves to others. Misguided, we will often prepare for holiness by trying harder or by checking off a lengthy "to do" list to make it happen. Our attempts create illusions of holiness—shadows of the divine. Ultimately, they are empty and unattainable. However, God wants us to draw near to Him, to long for intimacy, and to surrender to His divine will. The fact is, it is much simpler that way—not necessarily easier, but simpler.

As we seek holiness, let our justification only come from Jesus Christ. Each of us may choose to spend some time with Him and say, "God, I've been trying to come off looking better than I am. I've been trying to work my way into your approval when You already love me dearly. I've been trying to win arguments, find pleasure, gain wealth, or keep it all together without you. Let me simply and honestly show others who You have made me to be. Let me simply and honestly love people so that every word that proceeds from my mouth will be glorifying to You. Let me simply and honestly rely on Your daily graces and seek an intimacy with You that is beyond measure. Help me to do this not because I am a person of great integrity, but because I am a child of Yours and because Your nature is growing in me, not my own self-righteousness."

The path to holiness is simple. Jesus Christ has already paved it for us. But it is impossible to trek without the nature of Christ growing in us. The only hope we have is in Jesus Christ because He loved us enough to die for us.

His love is great enough for us to rest in grace each day. His love is great enough that we can relinquish control and yield to Him. His love is great enough that we can love others deeply. His love is great enough that we can love Him in return. His love is enough that we are compelled to kneel before Him—for He is holy.